Preaching Through the Bible

Joel and Amos

Michael Eaton

Sovereign World

Sovereign World
PO Box 777
Tonbridge
Kent, TN11 0ZS
England

By the same author:
Ecclesiastes (Tyndale Commentary) – IVP
Living A Godly Life – Paternoster
Living Under Grace (Romans 6–7) – Paternoster
Predestination and Israel (Romans 9–11) – Paternoster
Enjoying God's Worldwide Church – Paternoster
A Theology of Encouragement – Paternoster
Applying God's Law – Paternoster
1 Samuel (Preaching Through the Bible) – Sovereign World
2 Samuel (Preaching Through the Bible) – Sovereign World
1, 2 Thessalonians (Preaching Through the Bible) – Sovereign World
Mark (Preaching Through the Bible) – Sovereign World
Genesis 1–11 (Preaching Through the Bible) – Sovereign World
1, 2, 3 John (Focus on the Bible) – Christian Focus
Hosea (Focus on the Bible) – Christian Focus
Experiencing God – Paternoster

ISBN: 1-85240-243-1

Typeset by CRB Associates, Reepham, Norfolk
Printed in England by Clays Ltd, St Ives plc.

General Preface

This is a further exposition in the series *Preaching Through the Bible*. It is the first one to be written on any of the prophets.

There is need of a series of biblical expositions which are especially appropriate for English-speaking people throughout the world. Such expositions need to be laid out in such a way that they will be useful to those who like to have their material or (if they are preachers) to put across their material in clear points. They need to avoid difficult vocabulary and advanced grammatical structures. They need to avoid European or North American illustrations. *Preaching Through the Bible* seeks to meet such a need. Although intended for an international audience I have no doubt that their simplicity will be of interest to many first-language speakers of English as well. These expositions are based upon the Hebrew and Greek texts. The New American Standard Version and the New International Version of the Bible are recommended for the reader but at times the expositor will simply translate the Hebrew or Greek himself. In this book a translation of Joel and Amos is provided.

It is not our purpose to deal with minute exegetical detail, although the commentator has to do work of this nature as part of his preliminary preparation. But just as a housewife likes to serve a good meal rather than display her pots and pans, so we are concerned with the 'good meal' of Scripture, rather than the 'pots and pans' of dictionaries, disputed interpretations and the like. Only occasionally will such matters have to be discussed. Similarly matters of 'Introduction' receive only as much attention as is necessary for the exposition to be clear. On occasions a simple outline of some 'introductory' matters will be included, perhaps in an appendix, but the first chapter of each exposition gets into the message of Scripture as speedily as possible.

Although on the surface written simply these expositions aim at a high level of scholarship, and attempt to put the theological and practical message of each book of the Bible in a clear and practical manner. Simplicity of style is not simplicity of content. God's word needs to be expounded with thoroughness but the language needs to remain easy and accessible. Some progress in this direction is attempted in these expositions.

Michael A. Eaton

Contents

Author's Preface

As always these chapters are based upon my preaching. My preaching through the Book of Joel at Rouxville Baptist Church, Johannesburg, plus my broadcasts on Joel for Trans-World Radio, my lectures on Joel at the Baptist Theological College, Johannesburg, my preaching in various meetings of the Chrisco Fellowship of Churches, four sermons on Joel at Westminster Chapel, London, on two Sundays a year apart – have all brought their contributions to these chapters.

Recently I have been preaching on Amos in the Chrisco Intensive Discipleship School, Nairobi. It was a colourful time in Kenya's history. The nation was eager to see what would happen as we went into a new phase of history with various reforms added to the law-books. I began preaching on Amos on 10 November 1997 under the heading 'What Kind of a Nation Do We Want?' Some massive prayer meetings were held in our capital city. The national elections were on 29–30 December 1997. Most of the local application is cut out of this book; only the central exposition of Amos remains. But 'Amos' was the right book for that occasion. I finished the series in March 1998. As always I am grateful to friends and members of the family who have given help and support to my ministry in Nairobi and elsewhere.

Because this book is a book of preaching, the 'analysis' of Amos comes in along the pathway of the exposition. Preachers do well to tell the people how the book unfolds along the pathway of the exposition and with periodic reminders.

Preachers have to have one foot in the scholarly world, and scholars need to keep their eye on the practical needs of the church's preaching. Luther's work as a preacher has always been an inspiration to me in this connection. He did not differentiate between his lectures in the classroom and his messages in the church. The pulpit, for Luther, was a kind of popular professorial chair! And when he was at Wittenburg University, the professorial chair was a kind of students' pulpit. Luther's preaching was high in content; it was not so different from his lecturing. Luther's lecturing was high on application to the living situation of Luther's day; it was not so different from his preaching.

Luther retained the freedom of the Holy Spirit. It is obvious reading his lectures today that he did not know precisely at what point his material would come to an end. When he was preaching he did not write out his manuscript in full. He had a written outline and no more. Skevington Wood says 'Occasionally he even forgot his line of thought and preached a better sermon than he had intended'. 'Our Lord God Himself wishes to be the preacher', said Luther. 'It has often happened that my best outline came undone. On the other hand, when I was least prepared my words flowed during the sermon'. Luther has been a model for me, in this respect. 'The church is not a pen house, but a mouth house. For since the advent of Christ the gospel which used to be hidden in the Scriptures, has become an oral preaching. And thus it is the manner of the New Testament and of the gospel that it must be preached and performed by word of mouth and a living voice. Christ Himself has not written anything, nor has He ordered anything to be written, but rather to be preached by word of mouth'. For me, preaching is prior to writing; and writing is the write-up of preaching. Amos was a preacher first; then we got Amos' book. My own writing comes into being in the same way.

Michael A. Eaton

Chapter 1

A Time to Seek the Lord

(Joel 1:1–3)

There are times in life when something happens to us which for us is like the end of the world. There came a time in Israel's history when there was a plague of locusts so terrible that it seemed to be the end of the world for Israel. It went on for several years. It ruined the agriculture of Israel. Food supplies sank to zero.

At this time God raised up a preacher called 'Joel', who was led by God to make this plague of locusts the theme of his preaching. We do not know exactly when he did this preaching. Some think that it was in the reign of Joash at about 835 BC. We do not know for sure. What is more important for us is to note the circumstances in which Joel was preaching.

Like all of the prophets, Joel was a preacher, and this book of the Bible is a record of his preaching. The nation of Israel was in a terrible situation. Joel sees the hand of God in what is happening and calls the nation to repentance. He sees this locust plague as a foretaste of the end of the world. He is led by God to see that there is a special reason why God has let this plague of locusts come upon them. It is God's warning to them. An intervention into the normal course of life could come at any time. The Day of the Lord – God's judgement day – is always near. Joel urges the people to seek the Lord in a way they have never done before. Then Joel is led by the Spirit to widen his theme, and to talk of the Day of the Lord in a fuller way.

No particular sin is mentioned in Joel's prophecy. There is no mention of idolatry or social sins. He mentions drunkenness passingly in Joel 1:5 but it was not the aim of Joel to denounce any one particular misdeed. Evidently Joel was concerned more about general negligence of the people in the things of God. This plague of locusts gave the nation an opportunity to wake up to spiritual reality.

First there is the title (Joel 1:1).

Then there comes a summons to the nation (Joel 1:2–2:17). Joel addresses every section of the community (1:2–14). He calls upon the elders (1:2–4), the drunkards (1:5–7), Jerusalem (1:8–10), the farmers (1:11–12), the priests (1:13–14). He calls the whole nation a section at a time. He tells them what to say (1:15–20). He puts a cry of repentance in their mouths.

Then there comes a second summons to the nation in Joel 2:1–17. The locust plague is being used as a picture of the Day of the Lord. Joel is describing the final great day of the Lord as though it was a very great plague of locusts. The picture of a locust plague is taken up by the prophet and used as a way of picturing judgement day. Joel now refers to 'the nations' (2:6) and 'the earth ... sky ... sun ... moon ... stars' (2:8). In Joel chapter 1 he had mentioned only the local scene.

Joel 2:18–3:21 deal with mercy and judgement in the Day of the Lord. Joel widens his message. He applies what he has said to the whole world, as well as the situation in Israel. God will remove the judgement of the locusts and bless Israel. They will be restored materially (2:18–27). Then 'afterwards' the Spirit will be poured out (2:28–32). God will provide for the world spiritually as well as materially. Salvation will come to Jerusalem. In Joel chapter 3 he speaks of the judgement which comes upon all of the nations.

1. In the book of Joel we must remember that **we are dealing with the Word of God**. It begins: *'The word of the Lord that came to Joel, the son of Pethuel'* (1:1). There is no mention of any king. Joel could have been written in the reign of a young king like Joash or it could have been written at the time when there were no kings (after the exile). Personally I think the book is early rather than late.

The important thing is that this title makes the claim that Joel's book is the word of God. 'The word of the Lord came ... ' The prophets make this claim. Their message is for their own day, but by the Holy Spirit they are given something wider. It is not just Joel's thinking that we have in this book.

It is the 'Word of the Lord'. God revealed something to him. This is the claim of the Bible. Joel's words are God's Word. The whole Bible is like this. Paul said of the Old Testament, *'All Scripture is God-breathed'* (2 Timothy 3:16). He was referring to the Old Testament but the same thing is true of the whole Bible.

The Bible has a double authorship. Joel wrote his book, but God was behind it as well. The Spirit illumined Joel's mind. There are predictions, glimpses of the future (for example in 2:28). Joel is saying something on behalf of God.

2. **Sudden interruptions in life's routine are often a call from God**. Joel starts his central message:

'Hear this, you elders,
and listen, all inhabitants of the land.
Has anything like this happened in your days
or in the days of your forefathers? (1:2)
Tell it to your children,
and let your children tell it to their children,
and their children to the next generation.' (1:3)

When God steps into your life with something unusual you should always take notice. The plague was unusual ('Has anything ever happened like this . . . ?') It was very serious. The nation had run out of grain. When God intervenes in a striking way into one's life one should take notice.

We tend to think that life will go on as it has always been. But life is not like that. There come interruptions, things that move you out of the run of normal routine. A crisis wakes us up, and should lead us to turn to God. We should learn the lesson and pass on what we have learned. We tend to get careless but then something happens and shakes us out of our complacency. That is a time to seek the Lord. We should try to learn the lessons of events that are unusual ('Tell it to your children . . . '). Learn the lesson and pass it on. Let the next generation learn something because you learned something from the Lord in a time of crisis. Are you shaken out of your normal routine? Then it is time to seek the Lord.

Chapter 2

Blessing Through Crisis

(Joel 1:4–7)

The plague of locusts went on for several years. It progressively ruined the nation. It destroyed the agriculture. There was no food for the people. It affected the temple-worship. The grain for grain-offerings and drink-offerings were 'cut off' (1:9). Joel sees this as coming from God. God controls whatever happens. He had allowed this terrible thing to wake them up from their carelessness.

Do you know what it is to get careless with regard to the things of God? You cease to be careful about the way you live or think or act. General negligence creeps into your life. This had happened in Israel. Joel does not deal very often with specific sins. He deals more with general carelessness. Interventions in the routine of life are always significant. God may allow something unusual to wake us up. He can intervene in mercy, or in judgement. He can do something which is wonderful – or something that is awesome which makes us aware of God in a new way. God breaks traditions. 'Has this ever happened before?' asks Joel.

We should take notice when something unusual happens – whether it is wonderful or whether it is disturbing.

> '*. . . Has anything like this happened in your days*
> *or in the days of your forefathers?* (1:2)
> *Tell it to your children,*
> *and let your children tell it to their children,*
> *and their children to the next generation.*' (1:3)

The Bible is interested in the story of the people of God. Christians should be interested in what God has done in days gone by. Joel envisages that future generations will learn from what happened in Joel's day. Joel's preaching got put into writing and we are learning from what happened even today.

God's chastening often takes the form of some kind of deprivation. When crisis comes it is God's way of speaking. We do not always like it. In Joel's day, God allowed the crops to be devastated. There was one swarm after another of locusts. They came in wave after wave, and destroyed everything edible. They damaged the vines. The people could not make wine any more. They were deprived of the necessities of life. The crops were ruined (1:11). It affected the whole agriculture of the nation.

'What the locust swarm has left
the great locusts have eaten;
what the great locusts have left
the young locusts have eaten;
what the young locusts have left
other locusts have eaten.' (1:4)

We learn then: chastening sometimes takes the form of deprivation of something you feel you need. God can remove something from you, not because He is angry or bitter, but because He wants you to think. He is capable of withdrawing a basic necessity for your life. It could be something in the realm of money. God can withdraw your supplies, if you are careless about the things of the Lord. He can withhold success or honour. He can withhold vindication; you find you cannot prove you are right in some quarrelsome situation.

The reason why God handles us severely is to get us to think about what is happening in our lives. He wants us to be saved and to be living for Him. If it takes severity before we take God seriously, then God can act in severity. The nation was getting careless. The crisis did not last for ever. God changed the situation after a year or so. It was a temporary withholding of the necessities of life.

'Wake up, you drunkards, and weep!
and wail, all you wine drinkers,
wail because of the new wine
that is snatched from your lips.' (1:5)

It is almost amusing. The drunkards of the nation used wine, but God can remove the very thing you use to sin with. It was 'snatched' from their lips. He can do anything. The very thing you use to sin with, He can take away. He is all-powerful. His powerful chastening is part of His mercy.

'For a nation has invaded my land,
powerful and too great to be numbered.
Its teeth are the teeth of a lion,
and it has the fangs of a lioness. (1:6)
It has made my vine a ruin,
and my fig-tree a stump of dead wood.
It has stripped them bare and thrown them away;
their branches have become white.' (1:7)

The nation was devastated (v. 4). It was facing starvation. In verse 6 the coming of the locusts is described as being like a nation of invaders. (This refers still to the locusts.) They were powerful and innumerable. They laid waste the vines. They stripped the bark off the trees, leaving only the white tree underneath.

God's calling us to consider Him can be sudden. 'Snatched away' (v. 5) speaks of suddenness. God can do this to get us to respond to Him. He is not severe because He enjoys it. The point of His severity is that He might restore us, to get us to come back to Him. He disciplines us and this upsets us and makes us alarmed. Yet it is God's way of getting us to seek Him.

Are you drifting from God? Is God allowing things to happen to you that get you to seek Him? We all find it easier to seek God when we are in trouble. It is a pity that we have to have trouble to get us to seek Him, but often that is the way it is. This can happen to individuals, to one person. It can happen to the whole church. Joel calls upon the whole of society. Elders (1:2), drunkards (1:5), Jerusalem (1:8), farmers (1:11), priests (1:13). He calls the whole nation. He began with the leaders because they ruled over the smaller units of the nation. They are to take the initiative.

Chastening does not have any value unless you understand it. This is what the book of Joel is all about. God sent Joel and he is preaching about this crisis, telling the nation what the crisis is, and what they should do. He addressed every section. There is a message from God explaining the crisis. There are two things at the same time. There is the catastrophe; and there is also the prophet, Joel addressing the nation. This is

God's way of getting through to them. He may allow something to happen to you. But at the same time He sends a word, a preacher. Seek the Lord. Turn to Jesus. Jesus died for all of your sins. Approach God through Jesus and His blood. Ask God 'What do you want me to learn from this crisis?' 'What would you have me learn from this blessing?' You will discover the Lord in a fresh way. That is what Joel wants to happen. Anything unusual that happens in your life is a prompting to seek Him in a fresh way.

Chapter 3

Seeking the Lord

(Joel 1:8–14)

We have seen how God can use a crisis to wake up His people when they become careless. When this happens God calls upon responsible people to lead the community in prayer and bring the matter to Him. Joel addresses the elders (1:2), the people of the capital city, Jerusalem (1:8), the farmers (1:11) and the priests (1:13) – and the drunkards also (1:5)!

1. Joel has **a word for the leaders of society in the city of Jerusalem** (Joel 1:8–10).

'Wail like a girl dressed in sackcloth
grieving for the husband of her youth.' (1:8)

Verse 8 is dealing with the city of Jerusalem. Often in the prophets the city of Jerusalem is addressed as though the city were a young woman. Often Jerusalem is called 'the daughter of Zion' (as in 2 Kings 19:21; Lamentations 2:13).

Why does he specially address the 'daughter of Zion'? Jerusalem is the capital city. It is a place of responsibility. The temple is there. During the times of the kings, the king would be there, and his palace. The high priest would be there.

Jerusalem was the place of leadership. The Bible always expects that leaders should take the lead. Joel calls upon the leaders. He referred to the elders in Joel 1:2. They should take a lead in spiritual matters. Jerusalem is addressed because it is an important place in Israel; the inhabitants should take a lead in turning to the Lord. He expects that these leaders will have a concern for the spiritual welfare of the people. Joel is especially concerned that the spiritual life of the country is suffering.

'The grain offering and the drink offering are cut off
from the house of the LORD.
The priests mourn,
those who minister before the LORD.' (1:9)

This plague of locusts affected the crops and that in turn affected the temple. In the temple there would be various offerings and these needed grain and wine. But both the grain and the vines (from which the wine came) were affected by the locusts.

We should always be concerned at events in the life of our friends or our church or our nation which affect spiritual life.

Different offerings in the days of Joel and the Mosaic law expressed different things. The burnt offering expressed self-consecration. The grain-offering spoke of the consecration of one's work and one's home. It took a lot of preparation at home. Every morning and every evening there was a burnt offering offered to God. But with it was the grain offering, speaking of the consecration of one's labour. And there was the drink offering, which spoke of one's willingness to pour out one's life to God.

The leaders are also to be concerned for the well-being of the agriculture and the countryside. Joel says:

'The field is ruined,
the land mourns,
for the grain is ruined,
the new wine dries up.
Fresh oil fails.' (1:10)

The people were suffering and Joel expects that the leading people in the city of Jerusalem should take note and should seek God on behalf of their country and the people they lead.

So there are three principles here. (i) Leaders should lead. Joel wants the city of Jerusalem to act. (ii) Leaders should notice what is happening and take responsibility. No one is a good leader if he does not take the initiative. (iii) The leaders' responsibility involves seeking God.

2. In the next two verses (Joel 1:11–12) Joel addresses **the commercial leaders of the land, the farmers**:

'Be ashamed, you farmers.
Wail, you vine growers
for the wheat and the barley;
because the harvest of the field is destroyed. (1:11)
The vine is dried up,
and the fig-tree is withered.
The pomegranate, the palm, and the apple tree –
all the trees of the field are destroyed,
and the rejoicing of the people is withered away.' (1:12)

The principle here is: you are responsible for the area of life where God has specially put you. Think of the situation here. The locusts affected the land and the agriculture. Now the farmers were specially involved in this. They were responsible for the feeding of the country and provision of grain and wine for the temple services. If this problem specially concerns the area of life in which they are involved, then they should specially be turning to the Lord in prayer. The principle is: you are responsible for the area of life where God has put you.

People are suffering: *'the rejoicing . . . is withered away'*. The farmers are specially involved with what is happening and what is causing the suffering of the people. So they specially must take responsibility and seek God's mercy and help.

3. Joel 1:13–14 address **the spiritual leaders of the land** and especially the leaders of the worship and ministry in Jerusalem: **the priests**.

They are to lead the nation in repentance. Sackcloth is a sign of repentance. It was very rough to wear, because it was made of goats' hair. It was a sign of seriousness with God.

'Put on sackcloth and mourn, O priests,
Wail, you who minister at the altar.' (1:13)

They must take time to seek God.

'Come, spend the night in sackcloth,
you ministers of my God . . .' (1:13)

They must consider their ways. They must think about the desperate plight they are in. If you really want to know God you must give Him time.

'. . . For the grain offering and the drink-offering
are withheld from your house of God.' (1:13)

They must get others involved.

'Consecrate a fast. Call an assembly.
Gather the elders,
gather all who live in the land,
to the house of the LORD your God...' (1:14)

They must be in great seriousness about this matter.

'...and cry to the LORD.' (1:14)

In the days we are in, after the coming of Jesus, we involve our Lord Jesus in all of this. We approach God through Jesus. In every time of crisis, every period of blessing, it is a time for seeking God in a special way, approaching Him through the blood of Jesus.

Chapter 4

The Day of the Lord

(Joel 1:15–20)

Joel has called the whole nation to prayer. The leaders of the land, in Jerusalem, and especially the priests are to see to it that the people turn to God. Joel sees this terrible plague of locusts as a time when 'the day of the Lord' is drawing near.

1. **Any crisis in life is a foreshadowing of the Day of the Lord.**

'Alas for the day!
For the day of the LORD is near.' (1:15)

What is this 'Day of the Lord'? We must remember that we are looking at a section of the Old Testament. We know about the Second Coming of Jesus, mentioned in the New Testament. In the Old Testament the teaching about the Second Coming of Jesus was not fully revealed. God revealed things in stages, a little at a time. If we are well-taught Christians we know of the teaching concerning the Second Coming of Jesus, the day when every eye shall see Him. But the Old Testament does not use the name Jesus. It does not describe in such detail everything we have in the New Testament. It is not as full as Matthew 24, 1 Thessalonians 4–5; 2 Thessalonians 2. The Old Testament believer has a less fully detailed glimpse of the Day of the Lord.

They had a conviction that there was so much wrong with the world that God would just have to step in, in some special way. They did not know much about how God would do it but they knew that God would step into history in some special way. They called that the 'Day of the Lord'.

There were in their understanding two aspects to God's intervention, two things that God would have to do. He would have to judge sin, and He would have to save the righteous.

There were no statements of time about this. It was an undated hope, an undated expectation.

This vision was a total vision. It was a 'panoramic' vision. A 'panorama' is a seeing of everything at the same time. Imagine standing at the top of a very high building and being able to see the whole city below. The Day of the Lord in the Old Testament takes in everything God will do beginning from where the prophet lives. So in Joel the Day of the Lord takes in at least four things. (i) It includes the locust plague in his own day. The Day of the Lord is right there in Joel's time. Joel's description in chapter 1 is the Day of the Lord. (ii) It includes the gospel age, and the outpouring of the Spirit. (iii) It includes things that would happen along the way. Joel 3:6, 8 refer to events that took place in the fourth century before Jesus. (iv) It includes the end of the world.

When the New Testament comes along you see more, and the stages are able to be seen. You see the distinction between the first Coming of Jesus and the Second Coming of Jesus. But in the Old Testament this is all seen in one sweep.

The end of the world can be foreshadowed. Consider this locust plague. It was a foreshadowing of the Day of the Lord. Joel sees the Day of the Lord in the locust plague. Now this is a very important biblical principle. Let me give you some other examples of it.

In the prophecy of Joel, the plague of locusts foreshadowed the Day of the Lord. In the prophecy of Obadiah the destruction of Edom foreshadowed the Day of the Lord. In the prophecy of Isaiah the end of Babylon foreshadowed the Day of the Lord. In Matthew chapter 24 the fall of Jerusalem foreshadowed the Day of the Lord.

Any crisis in life is a foreshadowing of the Day of the Lord. The principle is that of Obadiah 15. The Day of the Lord is near upon all the nations.

2. **A crisis gets us to see what the Day of the Lord is like**. This is the point of Joel 1:15–20. The people cry 'Alas for the Day!' It is right there. The characteristics of the final Day of the Lord are present.

There will be destruction of sin.

> *'And it will come as destruction from the*
> *Almighty.'* (1:15)

It will be marked by suddenness. Suddenly there was no food, no grain for the temple service.

'Has not food been cut off before our eyes?
Is not joy and gladness cut off from our house of
God?' (1:16)

Everything is affected by God's coming.

'The seed shrivels under the shovels.
The storehouses are desolate;
the barns are broken down.
For the grain is dried up. (1:17)
How the animals groan!
The herds wander aimlessly.
Because there is no pasture for them.
Even the flocks of sheep are suffering. (1:18)
To you, O Lord, I call,
for fire has devoured the pastures of the wilderness.
And the flame has burned up all the trees of the
countryside. (1:19)
Even the wild animals pant for you;
the streams of water have dried up,
and fire has devoured the pastures of the
wilderness.' (1:20)

Every aspect of life is affected, the worship (v. 16), nature, agriculture (v. 17), the animals (v. 18), the countryside (v. 20).

There is one difference between the final judgement day and any anticipation we may have of it. The final judgement day will leave no room for repentance. But when we experience God's judgements now, in our history, God leaves opportunity for repentance. When we get these crises in our lifetime God is calling upon us to seek Him and get close to Him through Jesus. God may give us a glimpse of the end of the world – before the end of the world. Yet God gives room for us to turn to Him to call upon the name of Jesus, to confess our sins, to admit anything God is saying to us. Then we are able to get right with God through Jesus – who died upon the cross for our sins.

Chapter 5

Getting Ready for God's Intervention

(Joel 2:1–12)

In chapter 2 Joel is continuing the theme of the Day of the Lord, only now he goes further. Once again he describes the Day of the Lord (2:1–11); and again he calls the people to seek the Lord (2:12–17). But this time he does so in a deeper way.

The relationship between chapter 1 and chapter 2 is this: the locust plague is being used as a picture of the Day of the Lord, at a higher level and in a greater way. He is describing the final great Day of the Lord as though it was a very great plague of locusts. The picture of a locust plague is taken up by the prophet and used as a way of picturing judgement day. The Book of Revelation does the same thing in Revelation 9:3, 7–11. In chapter 1 the background had been local. Now the outlook looks out on the entire universe. Now Joel refers to 'the nations' (2:6), 'the earth . . . sky . . . sun . . . moon . . . stars' (2:8).

1. **God's people are called to be ready for the Lord's intervention at any moment**.

'Blow the trumpet in Zion;
sound the alarm on my holy hill.
Let all who live in the land tremble,
for the day of the Lord is coming.
Surely it is near.' (2:1)

Remember the prophets' view of the Day of the Lord. The prophets had a conviction that there was so much wrong with the world that God would just have to step in, in some special way. They knew that God would judge sin and save the righteous. They did not give any dates concerning these matters. They had a vision of everything that God would do. They did not see any dates or times. The Day of the Lord can be foreshadowed. It is near upon all the nations. Every crisis gets us to see what the Day of the Lord is like. The judgement day is such a vast and terrible thing that all the Bible can do is use various pictures and metaphors to describe it.

The Day of the Lord is always near. Even if the end of the world is not at hand there can be a foretaste of the end of the world.

It is God's people Israel who ought to be ready. He refers to Zion (Jerusalem), the capital of God's people in pre-Christian times. The 'holy hill' was where the temple was. Others are careless and do not believe in God's interventions. They do not know of the Day of the Lord. God's people are called to be ready.

2. **In the Day of the Lord there is judgement and punishment of sin. There can be salvation too** (2:32), but God's intervention always exposes and punishes sin.

This day is:

'a day of darkness and gloom,
a day of clouds and thick darkness.' (2:2)

It is large and powerful:

'Like darkness[1] *spreading over the mountains,*
a large and mighty army comes,...' (2:2)

This still uses the language of a locust plague, but it describes any judgement. It is unique:

'...such as never was of old
nor ever will be in ages to come.' (2:2)

It is characterised by complete extermination. Verse 3 says:

'A fire consumes before them,
and behind them a flame burns.' (2:3)

'Before' and 'after' refer to totality.

It is devastating:

'Before them the land is like the garden of Eden;
but behind them it is like a desolate wilderness.' (2:3)

Verses 4–11 describe God's judgement as being like a terrible army of invaders.

'They have the appearance of horses; (2:4)
and they run like war horses.
With a noise like that of chariots

they leap over the tops of the mountains,
like the noise of a flame of fire consuming stubble,
like a mighty army arranged for battle. (2:5)
Before them the tribes are in anguish,
every face turns pale. (2:6)
They run like warriors;
they climb the wall like soldiers.
They all march in line,
not swerving from their course. (2:7)
They do not crowd each other;
they each go straight ahead.
They break through the defences,
they do not break ranks. (2:8)
They rush upon the city;
they run over the wall.
They climb into the houses
like thieves they enter through the window. (2:9)
Before them the earth quakes,
the sky trembles.
The sun and the moon grow dark,
and the stars lose their brightness. (2:10)
And the LORD utters His voice before His army.
Surely His forces are very great,
for strong is He who carries out His Word.
The Day of the Lord is great and terrifying.
Who can endure it?' (2:11)

Some of this is picture-language. Revelation 9:7–12 uses the same language. The judgements of God are like armies of locusts. In Joel's day the locust plague was so great that Israel went on using the language of a locust-plague afterwards when describing the judgements of God. Yet there are indications that Joel is using the locust plague to point to something bigger and greater. Joel refers to 'nations' in 2:6. There is reference to the world and the universe in 2:11. So we have had many pictures of judgement: darkness – invasion – fire – a garden becoming a desert – an army of locusts. This is all picture-language picturing God's terrible judgement.

3. **The way to escape God's imminent judgement is to get close to Him and turn from sin.**

'But even now, says the LORD,

turn to Me with all your heart,
with fasting and weeping and mourning.' (2:12)

Joel tells the people to get close to God. 'Turn to Me', says God. The way of safety in the midst of judgement is to be close to the Lord. They are to take time ('with fasting'). Fasting was a way of giving up the common activities of life in order to give time to seeking God. They are asked to face their sins till they see how awful sin is.

We also may get foretastes of judgement day. Crises come. What do we do? We turn to God. We do so through Jesus. Jesus died for our sins so that we might turn to God in the way Joel asks.

Footnote

[1] The word 'darkness' is 'dawn' in some translations. It is likely that the Hebrew *sh-ch-r* should be pointed *shechor* with shewa and cholem. The Masoretic text means 'dawn'; *shechor* means 'darkness'.

Chapter 6

Getting Close to the Lord

(Joel 2:12–17)

Joel is calling upon the people of Israel to turn to the Lord. Joel chapter 1, we remember, describes the locust invasion. In Joel 2:1–11 the prophet used this as a picture of the great judgements of God that take place in history. Now he calls upon the people to get close to God. It is a helpful passage when we feel we are a long way away from God.

1. **They are to get close to God Himself**. He does not ask them simply to turn to religion or to change their lives a little.

> *'But even now, says the* L*ORD,*
> *turn to Me with all your heart, . . .* (2:12)

Joel says 'Turn to God Himself'. They must have dealings with the Lord.

2. **They are to take time over this**. This is the point of the reference to fasting. They must come:

> *' . . . with fasting and weeping and mourning.'* (2:12)

Fasting is a way of giving time to seeking the Lord. They are to give up the regular activities of life in order to seek the Lord.

3. **They are to face the fact of their sins**. They must come 'with . . . weeping . . . mourning'. They are to think about what they have done. Does this mean that the Lord needs our tears? No, but the weeping is taking seriously what we have done, seeing the bitterness of it. If we do not face what we have done we are likely to do it again.

The order is important. It is 'turn . . . weep'. Not 'weep . . . turn'. We get back to God and then regret we did not do so sooner. This is a consistent order. We turn to God through Jesus. Jesus is not mentioned by name in the Old Testament, yet from the viewpoint of the New Testament we know that Jesus is the way to God.

4. **Joel asks for reality not ceremony**. He tells them:

'Tear your heart
and not your garments,
and turn to the LORD your God.' (2:13)

In Israelite public meetings for repentance, one thing that would be done would be the tearing of your clothes as a way of expressing your feelings. There was a danger of using this external ceremony without there being any corresponding reality in one's heart. Joel says: Don't let your repentance be a matter of public ceremony. Don't worry about symbolising repentance. What matters is the real thing not simply some ceremony. Don't be content with religious ceremonies. Joel knew that if they tore their garments but nothing was happening in their hearts, it would be of no value at all.

5. **They are to trust in God's mercy**. They are to hold on to the character of God.

'For he is gracious and compassionate,
slow to anger and abounding in love,
and He relents from sending calamity.' (2:13)

They are to remember what God is like as they go to the Lord in prayer. They hold on to what God's character is known to be. We remember God's mercy and love at such a time. Think of the Syrophoenician woman. She held on to Jesus's mercy: 'Even the dogs get some crumbs from under the table'. She was clinging to the mercy of God.

Consider the words used here. (i) God is 'Gracious'. This is God's free and undeserved graciousness. (ii) 'Compassionate'. This is feeling moved within because of someone's suffering. God is compassionate. When in trouble you can tell Him how you feel. (iii) God is 'slow to anger'. God does not act abruptly. (iv) Great in love. The word means both 'loyalty' and 'love'. God has a special relationship to his people. He does not lightly give up on someone He has a relationship with. This is the ground of the appeal. This is what the Lord is like. God does not act in judgement unless He really has to. Jesus holds on to you. He does not easily give up on you. Maybe you have brought down upon yourself the judgement of God. These things encourage you. God is gracious. He abounds in loyal love.

6. **They are to look to God to turn away from His judgements**. God 'relents over the evil'. God repents as well as us.

'Who knows? He may turn and have pity
and leave behind a blessing –
grain offerings and drink offerings
for the LORD your God.' (2:14)

They go to God in confession and expect God to turn away from His chastening. This is why God sent Joel. Joel speaks in order that the calamity might turn away. Why does God warn of judgements? In order that judgement might be averted. *'He may turn and have pity . . .'*. If they will turn to God there might come a great change.

7. **They are to involve the whole community in this turning to the Lord**.

'Blow the trumpet in Zion,
declare a holy fast,
call a sacred assembly. (2:15)
Gather the people,
sanctify the assembly;
bring together the elders,
gather the children,
those nursing at the breast.
Let the bridegroom leave his room
and the bride her chamber. (2:16)
Let the priests, who minister before the LORD,
weep between the temple porch and the altar.' (2:17)

Joel calls upon every section of the community. He is not thinking only of individuals. Individual believers can turn to God in this way but Joel is concerned about more than that. He calls upon everyone, even the children, and the newly married. When a community does turn to the Lord in this way, you have revival. This is what revival is. It is when many people in a community seek God in a new way. They put all other things aside to turn to God. Even if a mother is breast-feeding or a couple are newly married, they must still seek God in this way. The priests must take a lead also.

8. **Joel tells them what to pray**:

   'Let them say, "Spare your people, O Lord.
   Do not make your inheritance an object of scorn,
   a byword among the nations.
   Why should they say among the peoples,
   'Where is their God?' "' (2:17)

They are to plead their relationship to God *'Spare your people'*. They use God's name: 'O Lord'. This is the name that God got at the time of the Exodus when he saved Israel 'by the blood of the lamb'. They are to plead the honour of God's name. Why should unbelieving people say *'Where is their God?'* When you deal with God in this way, God hears you. He will heal the land, remove the chastening, pour out His Spirit upon the land. He restores, forgives, heals the wounds of your life. It all takes place because of Jesus. He – as we now know – is the One who makes it possible for us to know God.

Chapter 7

The Blessings of Spiritual Restoration

(Joel 2:18–27)

The people of Israel were in a desperate situation. There was a locust plague, which was so bad that it was seen as a foretaste of the Day of the Lord. The Day of the Lord can come at any time. This means that we do not know when it will be. It also means that there can be a foretaste of it. This locust-plague was a foretaste of the end of the world.

In such a time of judgement the thing to do is to seek the Lord. God's warning judgements are His way of calling us to seek Him. This is what the people did in Joel's time.

Now in verse 18 we read of the result. We read of what God did as His people turned to seek Him. It is a turning point in the book. The best translation is: 'The Lord became jealous . . .'. By the time Joel was written the story was over. The book is narrating what happened when the people turned to God as Joel had asked. The Revised Standard Version rightly translates *'Then the Lord became jealous for His land . . .'*. It is a narrative of what happened.

'The Lord became jealous for His land,
and He had pity on His people.' (2:18)

When it says God 'became jealous' it refers to God's determined love for His people – a love that will not allow a rival, a love that will protect and not allow anything to interfere with that love. We see here what happens when God restores His people.

1. **God reverses the crisis or the calamity that He had sent before**.

'The Lord answered and said
"I am sending you grain, and wine, and oil,
enough to satisfy you fully; . . ."' (2:19)

These are the very things that they had lost in the locust-plague. The chastenings of God do not go on for ever. God may discipline you. After the people had sought the Lord the crisis ended.

2. **God will not send that particular crisis again**. Joel continues:

' " . . . never again will I make you
an object of scorn to the nations." ' (2:19)

This particular plague of locust would not come back again. He never repeated this particular plague. God does not send the same crisis once you have passed the test and have learned your lesson. That particular calamity need not be feared.

3. **He totally undoes what had happened when He was chastening**. God says:

' "I will drive the northerner far from you,
pushing it into a parched and barren land,
with its front columns going into the eastern sea
and those in the rear into the western sea
and its stench shall go up,
its smell will rise." ' (2:20)

The 'northerner' refers to the locusts who came from the north. God got rid of them altogether. One lot were driven into the desert, another into the Dead Sea, another into the Mediterranean. He is totally undoing what had happened before.

God will do that for you. If He puts you through a time of chastening, after you have learnt your lesson He will undo the chastening.

4. **He leads His people into the joy of restoration**. They say (v. 20):

'Surely he has done great things.' (2:20)

He calls upon them to be free from fear. God will not go on holding their sinful ways against them. He totally restores the country that He had judged:

'Be not afraid, O land;
be glad and rejoice.
Surely the LORD *has done great things.'* (2:21)

He restores the animals:

'Be not afraid O wild animals, . . . ' (2:22)

Before in the locust plague even the animals had suffered.

He restores the countryside:
'for the open pastures are becoming green....' (2:22)
He restores the trees:
'The trees are bearing their fruit;
the fig-tree and the vine yield their riches.' (2:22)
He restores the people:
'Be glad, O people of Zion,
rejoice in the LORD your God,...' (2:23)

God is undoing all of the calamities He had brought before.
He brings the rains back:
'...for He has given you the autumn rain[1] *in righteousness.*
He will cause the rain to come down for you,
the autumn rains and the spring rains as before.' (2:23)
He restores all the crops:
'The threshing-floors will be filled with grain;
the vats will overflow with new wine and oil.' (2:24)
He makes up for the lost years:
'"I will restore to you the years that the locusts have eaten,
the great locust and the young locust,
the other locusts and the locust swarm,
my great army that I sent among you."' (2:25)

This is a wonderful promise. God blesses them so much that the blessing makes up for the lost years. Joel refers to a literal plague but the principle applies in any way in which we have lost years because of our sins. Maybe God allows something that drives us to prayer. When He restores He makes up for everything we have lost. The promise is fulfilled in modern ways also, as we seek the Lord. He is able to make up for lost years. Maybe you have wasted years. If you will turn to the Lord He will start to compensate for the years you lost.

He abundantly provides:
'"You will have plenty to eat, until you are full,..."' (2:26)
This leads to worship:
'"...and you will praise the name of the LORD your God,
who has worked wonders for you;
never again will my people be shamed."' (2:26)

It leads to a deepened knowledge of God:

'"Then you will know that I am in Israel,
that I am the LORD your God,
and that there is no other;
never again will My people be shamed."' (2:27)

Three things they will see in a greater way: (i) God's indwelling ('...you will know that I am in Israel...'); (ii) God's name ('the LORD' – the One who saves and keeps by the blood of the lamb'); (iii) His uniqueness ('...there is no other...').

These are the things that happen when God restores you and makes up for the years that you have lost.

Footnote

[1] Some translation have 'teacher' but I think 'rain' is the better translation. It is 'in righteousness' because the Law promised that when His people were obedient He would give them rain.

Chapter 8

The Blessings of the Holy Spirit

(Joel 2:28–29)

Joel's promises lead on to the great promise of the Holy Spirit.

> '"*And afterwards,*
> *I will pour out My Spirit on all people.*
> *Your sons and your daughters will prophesy,*
> *your old men will dream dreams,*
> *your young men will see visions.* (2:28)
> *Even upon My servants, both men and women,*
> *I will pour out My Spirit in those days.*"' (2:29)

We must keep in mind the context of this passage. Joel has been speaking of the judgement of God. The Day of the Lord drew near in a plague of locusts. The people turned to the Lord in repentance. Then God ended the chastening.

Now this leads into a prediction of something that will happen afterwards. God has blessed them materially. But there is more to come. There is a blessing that God will send that is more spiritual.

'*I will pour out my Spirit . . .*' says God. This word 'pour out' always refer to something large and abundant. You have this phrase in connection with the Holy Spirit in Isaiah 32:15; 44:3, 5; Ezekiel 39:29; Zechariah 12:10. It is used in connection with the Holy Spirit and in these cases it is always referring to the future. The Day of Pentecost was future from the viewpoint of the Old Testament prophets. In the New Testament this word comes in Acts 2:17, 18, 33; 10:45; Romans 5:5; Titus 3:6.

This is a prediction of what began on the Day of Pentecost when God introduced a greater level of the experiencing of the Holy Spirit than had ever been known before among the people of God.

It refers to the experience of the Spirit that Christians are meant to enjoy since the Day of Pentecost. It refers to something not known much in the Old Testament. It was predicted for 'afterwards'.

The Spirit will come upon 'all flesh'. What is meant by 'all flesh'? In the prophecy of Joel it is possible to see what is initially meant by this phrase. It refers to 'Sons ... daughters ... ' all types of people everywhere. It also means that one day even Gentiles would be saved and blessed by the Holy Spirit. When the Spirit was poured out (Acts 10–11), the progress of events made it clear that 'all flesh' would include even Gentiles.

The prophecy speaks of 'My Spirit'. This is the breath of God. In the New Testament this 'breath of God' is called 'the Holy Spirit'.

'Sons and daughters will prophesy'. Prophecy is speaking for God with words given by God (see Deuteronomy 18:18). The Holy Spirit will bring all sorts of people to see the will of God, and will enable them to speak for God, with words given by God.

They receive understanding from God by 'dream' and 'vision'. These were modes of receiving words from God. 'Vision' does not have to be visual. It refers to knowing God's will, in any way at all. Prophetic understanding was often called 'vision' whether there was anything to be seen or not. In the Old Testament God often spoke in vision and dream. This is Joel's way of predicting what will happen through the outpouring of the Spirit, when people will have a heightened knowledge of God's will.

This outpouring of the Spirit will bring into being a community where all sorts of people are to be found (*'sons ... daughters ... young ... old ... men-servants ... '*). In the Old Testament times, slaves experienced much discrimination. They were excluded from many of the privileges of Israel, but a day is promised when all this will change.

This prediction was initially fulfilled on the Day of Pentecost. What happened on the Day of Pentecost outclasses anything of the Old Testament level of knowing the Spirit. The Old Testament believer had many blessings of the Spirit. The Spirit led them to faith. Abraham is a model of salvation. David knew the Spirit in a permanent way (1 Samuel 16:13). The Old Testament believer knew something of the special blessings of the Spirit. People like Samson, the judges, Bazalel (who built the tabernacle) did their work by the Spirit. They knew something of the Spirit's resisting sin (Micah 3:8). But they looked forward to a day when the Spirit would be poured out in a richer and deeper way.

What is this New Testament level of the receiving of the Spirit? John's Gospel speaks of rivers of living water (John 7:37–39). 'This he said of the Spirit'. Romans 8:15–16 and Ephesians 1:13, 14 tell of assurance, joy, power, freeness in prayer, calling God 'Abba', experiencing the 'Spirit of truth'. This is the kind of thing Jesus was referring to in John 7:37–39. *'Let him come to Me and keep drinking . . . Out of his heart shall flow rivers of living water . . . the Spirit'.*

There are side-effects to the outpouring of the Spirit. One is that people experience equality. In the church of Jesus Christ the Spirit gives equality. The Spirit abolishes discrimination in the church of Jesus Christ. In the Old Testament there was favouritism towards Israel and within Israel. The law was for Jews. Men were favoured. The 'upper-classes' were favoured. Certain nationalities near Israel were excluded from the worship of the tabernacle.

But the coming of the Spirit abolishes these discriminations. The Spirit transcends divisions in the human race. Male and female, rich and poor are all open to the Spirit. Matters of race or nationality make no difference. Slaves and free, Gentiles and Jews – the Spirit is given to all who believe in Jesus. Old and young may equally know the will of God. Even a slave may know the outpouring of the Spirit. 'All flesh' is able to receive the Spirit. This happened historically. Gentiles came to know Jesus. The Spirit was poured out even on them. God blessed everyone everywhere – who knew Jesus. 'Can anyone keep these people from being baptised with water. They have received the Holy Spirit just as we have . . . ', said

Peter. This is why Galatians says there is neither male or female in Jesus Christ. 'If any person is thirsty, let him come to me and drink . . .'. If you keeping 'drinking' from Jesus you too will know these blessings of the Holy Spirit.

Chapter 9

The Shaking of the Universe

(Joel 2:30–32)

We must continue to remember the story behind the book of Joel. A plague of locusts came and for several years damaged the land. The wine-trade was ruined. The crops were damaged. The people were hungry. The temple sacrifices were not provided for. Joel calls upon the people to turn to the Lord. This is what they did. God blessed them. The people had experienced God's judgement and they had experienced His blessing after judgement.

Joel says this is a foretaste of the end of the world. Every calamity is a foretaste of the end of the world. The Day of the Lord is near upon all of the nations (Obadiah 15). The Day of the Lord is the time when God steps into history and saves His people and judges His enemies. There can be a foretaste of it and the locust plague was a preview of what it would be like in His judgement.

In Joel 2:28–32 we have a prediction of the Day of the Lord. Judgement and salvation are mixed up together. Afterwards – after the locust plague – the Spirit will be poured out. It goes on to say God will show wonders in the heavens, and so on.

Salvation and judgement are prophesied together. Part of it was fulfilled on the Day of Pentecost. Peter referred to Joel on the Day of Pentecost (Acts 2:17–21). Yet Joel goes on to speak of wonders in the heavens. This kind of language in 2:30–32 refers to God's judgements. **It is an important principle to see that salvation and judgement are predicted in the same prophecy**. Prophecy is like this. It sees a wide sweep of everything God will do. Joel is given a vision of everything God will do to put things right, and bring salvation and judgement to the world. Judgement and salvation are seen at the same time. As the prophecies are fulfilled they come to pass a bit at a time. They gradually unfold. The prophets saw a sweeping vision, but it unfolds stage by stage. It is important to understand prophecy in this way. The total vision in Joel 2:28–32 includes two aspects to what God would do. In fulfilment, the first thing was the outpouring of the Spirit but there are other aspects to be fulfilled. This is the principle in Acts 1:7 *'It is not for you to know the times or the seasons ... But you shall receive power ...'*. They were asking a question about prophecy. Jesus says: It is not for you to know times and seasons.

As another example, think of Isaiah chapter 11. It has a prediction which includes the birth of Jesus. It also deals with the final glory of the world. It begins with the coming of a Saviour but it ends with saying *'The earth shall be filled with the glory of God ...'*. The vision covers everything God would do. As history went forward first Jesus came, then salvation was achieved, then the Spirit was given. But the day when the earth will be filled with the glory of God has not yet come. The prophecies are often given all in one vision, but they are fulfilled in stages.

In Joel 2:28–29, Joel promised that after the end of the chastening there would come even greater blessing. The locusts were removed but God promises more, including a new level of experiencing the Spirit. Old Testament believers knew something of the Spirit, but the prediction was that one day the Spirit would come in a greater way. This would lead to a new ability to speak for the Lord – prophesying. It would lead to a knowledge of God's will. Visions and dreams were ways of getting to know God's will in Old Testament times. God promised a widening of the people of God, so as to include slaves ... men ... women ... sons ... daughters, every kind of person. In Old Testament times God's people were simply within one nation; few Gentiles were saved. But the coming of the Spirit leads to a widening of the people of God.

> *' "And I will show wonders in the heavens and on*
> *the earth,*
> *blood and fire and columns of smoke.* (2:30)

The sun will be to darkness,
and the moon into blood,
before the coming of the great and awesome Day
of the L*ORD*.'' ' (2:31)

This kind of language refers to violent and dramatic events in the history of the world. It is language taken from Old Testament stories. Think of the plagues of Egypt, in passages such as Exodus 9:22. There was thunder, lightening, rain, hail. Tremendous events took place in the earth and in the sky. Joel predicts similar events in the surrounding nations. This language is an Old Testament way of speaking of great upheavals in the history of the world.

Similar language is found elsewhere. On Mount Sinai, the law came with thunder, lightening, and a trumpet blast. Sinai was covered with thick cloud, and then with smoke. The smoke billowed up. The whole mountain trembled. Joel 2:30–32 reminds us of the exodus and the giving of the law. When Jesus died there was an earthquake and the tombs were opened. The sun was darkened for three hours. The language here is similar.

' "*And it shall be that all who call on the name of*
the L*ORD will be saved.*
For on mount Zion and in Jerusalem there shall be
deliverance,
as the L*ORD has said,*
among the saved ones whom the L*ORD calls.*" ' (2:32)

In the middle of these judgements there is a promise of salvation (2:32). In the midst of all that may happen, God offers a way of deliverance. Five things are specially to be noted.

1. Salvation comes by calling on the Saviour.
2. Salvation is calling on the name of the 'Yahweh' (or Jehovah, often translated LORD). This is the name which means 'the God who saves by the blood of the lamb'. It is the name God got for Himself at the time of the first passover events.
3. Salvation is for everyone.
4. Salvation takes place in Jerusalem – the place where Jesus died.
5. Salvation comes as God calls us. We call upon Jesus, because God calls us to do so.

Chapter 10

The Valley of Judgement

(Joel 3:1–8)

Joel chapter 3 is a vision of the judgements of God in the history of the world. The people had experienced the judgement of God in a plague of locusts, but they had turned to the Lord and so had experienced His blessing. These events led Joel to talk about the Day of the Lord and the end of the world.

Because the chapter is a vision, it has a lot of symbolic language. We read that God enters into judgement and brings the nations down to the 'valley of Jehoshaphat' (3:2). There is actually no place called the 'valley of Jehoshaphat'. The word 'Jehoshaphat' means 'the Lord judges'. It is a symbolic valley, a visionary valley. One must not try to read into it particular dates and places. It is a vision of all that God will do. It is a vision of what happens as the Day of the Lord approaches, and the Day of the Lord itself. God judges sins even before the final judgement day. Some of the sins referred to are very local sins. 'Tyre' and 'Sidon' (3:4) were nearby localities in the days of Joel. They were Philistine ports involved in slave-trading where Israelites were being sold as slaves. Joel sees these places being judged. It is a principle of prophecy that the prophets see all that God will do all in one glimpse. They see everything that God will do, all mixed up together.

What is the Day of the Lord? In this vision (1) **The Day of the Lord is a day when the people of God are restored.**

> '*"For behold in those days and in that time,*
> *when I restore the fortunes of Judah and*
> *Jerusalem, . . ."*' (3:1)

God works in such a way that He restores His people. We

may face terrible opposition. The church may sink to a low level. God may allow enemies to overrun His people. But the vision of the future was that God would restore the fortunes of His people. When God judges, His people are restored. When God deals with sin, at the same time He rescues His people. We should not take this politically. Before Jesus God's people were a nation – Israel. When Jesus came there was a change in the structure of God's people. *'The kingdom of God ... will be given to a people who will produce its fruit'* (Matthew 21:43). Jerusalem was destroyed. 'Israel' does not refer just to a political entity in the modern world. *'They are not all Israel who are descended from Israel'*, says Romans 9:6. Judgement Day is a day when God's people are restored. God has a way of stepping into the history of the world and restoring the fortunes of His people.

(2) **God takes the initiative in judging the nations.**

' "I will gather all the nations
and I will bring them down to the valley of
Jehoshaphat.
And I will enter into judgement with them
there, ..." ' (3:2)

This is a vision of all that God would do in the judgement of the world, beginning with the sins of Tyre and Sidon and going on to the end of the world. God takes the initiative. God is the Lord of history and at any time He can bring the nations into a valley of judgement. He can affect history. He initiates the events (*'I will gather ...'*). It often looks as though the nations are out of control. But God is the Lord of history. He is there and He can bring nations down into the valley of Jehoshaphat. He takes the initiative when He feels like it.

(3) **Notice what it is that gets judged**. It is sin against God's people. Joel says God comes in judgement

' "... on behalf of My people, Israel My
inheritance,
whom they scattered among the nations, and
shared out My land. (3:2)
They cast lots for My people.
They traded a boy for a harlot,
and sold a girl for wine that they might drink." ' (3:3)

God protects His people, and judges sins against His people. Two things are mentioned. (i) Grabbing land. 'Concerning my inheritance' refers to the land. Philistia and other nations took the inheritance. They would do terrible things to get hold of territory. (ii) Slavery. 'They cast lots for My people'. They would gamble over the slaves. They would sell a boy to use the money. They would sell a girl and use the money for getting wine. The sin was the sin of mistreating people. Certain cities were being used: Tyre ... Sidon ... Philistia. These were coastal cities where the slaves were sold. These cities will be judged, and the sins will be recompensed. The underlying sin is that of exploiting people. They would capture someone and care nothing of how that person felt. Such sins will be on the agenda in God's judgement. Anyone who treats a person as a thing, as unimportant, as insignificant, is vexing God. When people are exploited, where the poor are mistreated, God gets angry.

(4) **Back behind these sins is resentment against God**.

' "And what are you to Me, O Tyre and Sidon and
all the regions of Philistia?
Are you repaying Me for something I have done?
If you are paying Me back, I will swiftly and
speedily repay you for what you have done." ' (3:4)

The Philistines would capture Israelites. Are they doing it because they hate the people of God? Or is it that they are hostile to the God of the Bible? Often behind the ill-treatment that the people of God receive there is hatred of God Himself. 'The servant is not greater than his master'. They treated Jesus badly; they will do the same to His people. You are likely to receive the same treatment as Jesus received. In Old Testament times the nations surrounding Israel hated the God of Israel. The natural man does not like the God of the Bible. Human nature does not submit to God's law and cannot please God. Joel's vision sees that one day all nations will be in this valley of judgement and all of this sin is dealt with.

(5) **The judgements are very appropriate**.

' "For you took My silver and My gold and carried
off My beautiful treasures to your temples." ' (3:5)

This seems to be a reference to some invasion of the treasures of Jerusalem.

'"You sold the people of Judah and the people of
Jerusalem to the Greeks, in order to remove
them far from their territory. (3:6)
See, I am going to rouse them out of the places to
which you sold them, and I will return on your
own heads what you have done. (3:7)
I will sell your sons and daughters to the people of
Judah, and they will sell them to the Sabeans,
a nation far away". The LORD *has spoken.'* (3:8)

What the enemies of God had done will come back to them. The judgement will be very appropriate. The Philistines will receive back the treatment they gave out to others. God is able to judge in a very appropriate way. They experience the very things they have done. They sold Jewish people to the 'Greeks' (the Ionian colonies around the Aegean Sea). In the fourth century they themselves became slaves.

We must remember Joel 2:32 when Joel reminded us that in the middle of the judgements everyone who called upon the name of the LORD would be saved. There is salvation in the midst of the judgements of God. Jesus is the fulfilment of this prophecy.

Chapter 11

God's New World

(Joel 3:9–21)

Joel chapter 3 is a vision of all the judgements of history beginning with Joel's own day (see 3:4, 6) but also going on to the end of history. Tyre and Sidon sold Israelites into slavery; they came from Joel's own times.

1. **The judgements of God often come in the form of upheavals among the nations**. It may be in the form of war or political crisis of some kind.

> *'Proclaim this among the nations:*
> *Prepare for war!*
> *Rouse the warriors!*
> *Let all the fighting men draw near and attack.* (3:9)
> *Beat your ploughshares into swords*
> *and your pruning hooks into spears.*
> *Let the weakling say,*
> *"I am strong!"* (3:10)
> *Come quickly, all you nations from every side,*
> *and assemble there.*
> *Bring down your warriors, O Lord!'* (3:11)

Here is a summons to the nations to get ready for war. Often the judgements of God come in this form. Behind these events God is the Lord of history. He controls everything that happens among the nations of the world. Often He allows things to happen in such a way that it brings judgements into the nations.

> *'"Let the nations be roused:*
> *let them advance into the Valley of Jehoshaphat,*
> *for there I will sit*
> *to judge all the nations on every side."'* (3:12)

A judge always 'sits' in a courtroom. We have here a picture of God's sitting in judgement and showing His hatred of sin. Every judgement that takes place in history gives a little foretaste of the final outpouring of God's wrath at the end of the world.

God is a holy God. He hates sin. The wrath of God is being revealed from heaven against all ungodliness. Jesus had to come because the wrath of God is being revealed in history against all sin.

2. **The judgements of God come when sin has reached its fullness.**

' "Swing the sickle,
for the harvest is ripe." ' (3:13)

God's judgement comes when evil has been allowed to come to a head. (Genesis 15:16 says *'The sin of the Amorites has not yet reached its full measure'*.) It is like a crop growing. When sin is full-grown then God steps in in some way. This is how the judgements of God work in history.

' "Come, trample the grapes,
for the winepress is full
and the vats overflow –
so great is wickedness!" ' (3:13)

3. **The judgements of God are very terrible.**

'Multitudes, multitudes
in the valley of [God's] *decision!'* (3:14)

The 'valley of decision' is the envisaged valley of God's judgement against sin. Joel refers to the great numbers that are involved. In this vision he sees that eventually even the universe is included.

'For the day of the Lord is near
in the valley of [God's] *decision.* (3:14)
The sun and the moon will be darkened,
and the stars no longer shine.' (3:15)

When God finally judges even the universe is involved. The chapter is a vision of all the judgements of God. He refers to Tyre and Sidon but also to the end of the world.

'The Lord will roar from Zion
and thunder from Jerusalem;
the earth and the sky will tremble.' (3:16)

The picture is that of a lion ('The LORD will roar . . .'). God hates sin. He is like a roaring lion against sin.

4. **In the midst of the judgement there is salvation**.

'But the LORD will be a refuge for His people,
a stronghold for the people of Israel.' (3:16)

God always provides salvation in the midst of judgement. When His wrath is roaring against sin, He provides a provision for rescue. There was an ark in the midst of the flood. There were rescuing angels at the time of the judgement of Sodom and Gomorrah. There was the passover lamb when Egypt was judged. So here also in the midst of judgement a salvation is provided. Jesus is the salvation in the midst of judgement. Even now as judgements fall among the nations, there is a saviour in the midst. In the Old Testament they looked forward to salvation amidst judgement. The refuge is for 'His people' – those who will turn around in faith.

' "Then you will know that I,
the LORD your God,
dwell in Zion, My holy hill;
never again will strangers invade her. (3:17)
In that day the mountains will drip new wine,
and the hills will flow with milk;
all the ravines of Judah will run with water.
A fountain will flow out of the LORD's house
and will water the valley of acacias. (3:18)
But Egypt will be desolate,
Edom a desert waste,
because of violence done to the people of Judah,
in whose land they shed innocent blood." ' (3:19)

These verses describe God's coming salvation. There comes a new world ('the mountains drip new wine'). This is God's final salvation.

There comes into being a new Jerusalem (*'Zion, My holy hill'*). We are not to think of this in political terms. It comes in Old Testament language but it refers to a 'Jerusalem' in which there is no sin. It cannot be touched by sinful people outside of God's people (*'never again will strangers invade her'*). The New Testament tells us of the 'new Jerusalem' where all believers are, and there is no sin.

It includes physical restoration. *'In that day the mountains will drip new wine, and the hills will flow with milk; all the ravines of Judah will run with water'*. The ultimate hope is a new earth (2 Peter 3:13). After God's final judgement day the old world is burned up and there comes into being a new world altogether, in which there is righteousness. The very territory of the universe is restored.

'A fountain will flow out of the LORD's house; and will water the valley of acacias'. Earlier we had the valley of Jehoshaphat – the valley of judgement. Now it is the valley of acacias – a beautiful tree. This is a picture of a flourishing world in which sin has been dealt with.

God's enemies are judged. Egypt will be a desolation, Edom a desert waste. 'Edom' stands for God's enemies. Joel thinks in terms of his own day. He thinks of the equivalent of Edom in the final judgement day. It must be taken spiritually. The ultimate vision is that all enemies are put down. God is eternally with His people. Judgement comes 'because of violence done to God's people' and then God is with His people. All of their sins are forgiven.

' "Judah will be inhabited for ever
and Jerusalem through all generations. (3:20)
Their bloodguilt, which I have not pardoned,
I will pardon."
The LORD dwells in Zion!' (3:21)

In Old Testament days this was true of the earthly Jerusalem. In the final state, the Zion is a heavenly Zion, God dwelling with His people for ever.

So this vision is a vision of all that God will do in judgement beginning with Joel's day and going on till the end of the world. It all takes place through Jesus. It was Jesus who was the salvation in Jerusalem. It is Jesus who will be the LORD dwelling among His people for ever!

Chapter 12

One Sin Too Many

(Amos 1:1–5)

The nation of Israel was established firmly through the exploits of king David just after 1000 BC. Israel's third king, Solomon, enjoyed a period of peace, inheriting the benefits achieved by his father David. But disaster struck the nation after Solomon's death when the nation divided into two. There was Judah in the south, and 'northern' Israel.

The prophet Amos preached about two centuries later at a time when two powerful kings were ruling the two nations. Uzziah (779–740) ruled Judah, and Jeroboam II (783–743) was king of northern Israel. Four things ought to be known about this period. (i) Both in the north and the south these were days of economic stability. (ii) They were also days of military danger. The Assyrians to the north were ambitious to extend their territory. (iii) They were days of social injustice. (iv) They were days of religious idolatry.

Alongside the kings were the prophets. Perhaps the first writing prophet was Obadiah in the 840s BC. Next may have been Joel in the days of Joash of Judah (835–796 BC). Jonah lived in the eighth century. Amos' short period of preaching was at about 760 BC or maybe earlier. Hosea was his contemporary. The prophets' writings are mainly their sermons to the nations of Israel, Judah, and their neighbours.

In the book of Amos, first of all we have a title. *'The words of Amos, who was one of the sheep-raisers from Tekoa, which he saw concerning Israel in the days of Uzziah the king of Judah, and in the days of Jeroboam son of Joash the king of Israel, two years before the earthquake'* (1:1).

Next we have the theme of this section of Amos:

'And he said:
"Yahweh has roared like a lion from Zion,
and from Jerusalem He has given forth his word,
and the pastures of the shepherds are in mourning,
and the peak of Carmel is withered."' (1:2)

In 1:3–2:16 Amos develops his point, presenting God's message to eight nations.

1. **God takes notice of all the nations as well as of Israel**. God is God of the whole universe and not merely the God of Israel or of the church. So in Amos 1:3 to 2:16 we notice that God not only addresses Israel and Judah, He has something to say about the surrounding nations as well. There are messages for Syria (1:3–5), Philistia (1:6–8), Tyre (1:9–10), Edom (1:11–12), Ammon (1:13–15), Moab (2:1–3), Judah (2:4–5) and then Israel (2:6–16).

2. **God's message to the nations was and still is a message of anger**. In these chapters God is presented like a roaring lion about to pounce upon the nations and devour them. The word 'roar' is the same as the one used in Judges 14:5 when a lion attempted to leap upon Samson. God gets angry with sin. He can destroy rulers (1:4) and buildings (1:4) and cities (1:5). He can send whole communities into exile (1:5). There is such a thing as the anger of God against sin. God's anger is His reaction to what is evil. This is why the world needs the gospel of Jesus Christ. *'The wrath of God is revealed from heaven against all ungodliness and unrighteousness of people who hold down the truth in unrighteousness'* (Romans 1:18). Many people try to avoid talking about the wrath of God. But the wrath of God is a fact of the Bible. For those with eyes to see it is a fact today. God hates sin and reveals His wrath against it in the events that are going on all around us. God responds to sin with indignation, with animosity, with determination to punish. God's wrath is His holy hatred of sin; it is His revulsion, His determination to act and wipe out sin from His universe. His wrath is seen (for those who can see it) in pestilence (see Ezekiel 14:19), in military devastation (Ezekiel 5:15), in drought (Deuteronomy 11:17), in plagues (2 Samuel 24:1ff).

When the Pharisees did not want a man healed on the

Sabbath, Jesus *'looked over them with anger, deeply grieved at the hardness of their hearts'* (Mark 3:5). It was not bad temper; it was Jesus' powerful angry grief at the callous sinfulness of the human race. He gazed with distressed outrage towards those men who did not wish a fellow human being to come to relief and comfort. And when we see Jesus like this we see the Father. This is the wrath of God against sin.

God's anger comes out of Zion. Amos says 'Yahweh has roared like a lion from Zion ... from Jerusalem ...'. The temple was in Jerusalem. Inside the temple was the place where God revealed His holiness. The ark inside the temple was like a throne. Today God's throne is only in heaven but in Amos' day there was a symbol of it in Jerusalem. *'The wrath of God is revealed from heaven ...'*. Our God is 'Yahweh' – the God who saves by the blood of a lamb. But He is also a roaring lion who hates sin and will pounce upon it sooner or later.

When God gets angry, His anger touches everything. *'The pastures of the shepherds are in mourning, and the top of Carmel is withered'* (1:2). From the low grasslands to the highest peaks, God's anger is over the entire land.

God's patience can discontinue. We must notice the precise way God speaks.

> *'This is what Yahweh has said:*
> *"For three transgressions by Damascus,*
> *and especially for four, I will not reverse my*
> *decision ..."'* (1:3)

This *'three transgressions ... and especially for four'* is a way of saying that God is very patient but eventually His patience can discontinue. A nation sins; God is patient. The nation sins again; God is still patient. The nation sins a third time; God is getting vexed. He determines that He will not be patient much longer. Then the nation sins a fourth time. It is enough. God is now determined to act. He makes up His mind and will not change it. Sometimes sin gets so bad and so persistent, God's patience runs out. God says, I will not reverse My decision. If I understand 3:4 rightly (see the exposition further ahead) the 'fourth transgression' has not been committed yet. The lion is roaring (see 1:2; 3:4a) but the prey has not yet been taken (see 3:4b). There is opportunity for repentance, but if the third transgression becomes the fourth transgression, the lion will not be roaring. He will growling contentedly over the dead meat.

What makes God angry with Damascus is their unjust violence. 'I will not reverse my decision', says God . . .

> '. . . *because they threshed Gilead with iron*
> *sledges.'* (1:3)

The Aramean state with its capital at Damascus had savagely attacked the area in Israel called Gilead. 'Threshing' seems to be a metaphor for savage treatment. Hazael the king of Damascus had treated people wickedly. It was as if he had laid people on the ground and driven over them with threshing tractors! God hates needless violence, and will eventually act against it.

> *' "So I will send fire against the house of Hazael,*
> *and it will consume the citadels of Ben-Hadad.* (1:4)
> *And I will break the gate-bar of Damascus,*
> *and I will cut off the sovereign from Biq'at-Awen,*
> *and the sceptre-wielder from Beth-Eden –*
> *and the Aramean people will go into exile to Qir."*
> *Yahweh has spoken!'* (1:5)

God will punish the capital city, Damascus. The fire of His holiness will exterminate the royal line of Hazael in the state of Aram. The fortresses will be destroyed. The capital city will be broken into. The king will be removed from the palace at Biq'at-Awen. The province of Beth-Eden will no longer have a ruler. The Aramean people will go into exile to Qir, where they came from originally. No one knows where Qir is but Amos' prophecy was fulfilled a few years later (see 2 Kings 16:9). The word of God was fulfilled but Amos had given them warning.

Chapter 13

The Roaring Lion

(Amos 1:6–10)

Amos continues to portray the roars of the roaring lion, about to pounce upon the nations surrounding Israel. Amos looks around at the nations near Israel and announces God's judgement against them. Damascus was condemned for its inhumane treatment of Gilead (1:3). In 1:6–10 two more nations are addressed.

What makes God angry with the Philistines is their using people for profit. Philistines were condemned for kidnapping whole communities in order to sell them as slaves. Moving from the north-east (Aram) to the south-west (Philistia) Amos next addresses Gaza, the mightiest Philistine town, and three other Philistine towns (Ashdod, Ashkelon and Ekron).

'This is what Yahweh has said:
"For three transgressions by Gaza,
and especially for four, I will not reverse my
decision.
Because they took into captivity an entire
community,
to hand them over to Edom."' (1:6)

There had been times when the Philistines had attacked Israel with the purpose of carrying off whole villages as slaves (as the Amalekites did to Ziklag in 1 Samuel 30:1–2). This would probably be part of an organised effort on the part of Israel's enemies.

God will soon act in judgement against the Philistines.

'"So I will send fire against the walls of Gaza,
and it will consume its citadels. (1:7)

And I will cut off the sovereign from Ashdod,
and the one who wields the sceptre I will cut off
from Ashkelon;
and I will bring back my hand against Ekron,
and the Philistines will perish even to the
remnant."
My Lord Yahweh has spoken!' (1:8)

God's punishment would be to wipe out of existence the defences of the city. The king would die. The population would be wiped out. Let us apply what Amos says to ourselves.

1. **The wickedness Amos mentions is a matter of disregarding the sacredness of people**. The Philistines were using people as things, disregarding the sufferings that were involved in slavery. They were putting commerce and profit above compassion and mercy. Part of the wickedness of the human race is our ingrained habit of self-centredness. So preoccupied do men and women become with our own interests and our own advantage, we begin to disregard altogether the claims of entire communities, ignoring what others are going through while we get what we want. We all are self-centred in this way to a lesser or greater degree. But it makes God angry.

2. **When God's anger is roused, He may take against us an irreversible decision of judgement**. *'For three transgressions . . . and especially for four, I will not reverse my decision'*. There comes a point when God is so roused to anger, after He has been patient for so long, that He eventually says *'I will not reverse my decision'*. Once a decision of this nature has been taken, God's judgement cannot be stopped.

3. **God's anger expresses itself in eventual extermination**. The words here clearly speak of some kind of annihilation. *'I will send fire against the walls of Gaza, and it will consume its citadels'* (1:7). *'Consuming fire'* clearly leaves nothing remaining. The Philistines *'perish even to the remnant'*. Not the slightest remainder of their community will be allowed to survive.

The next community to be addressed is the Phoenicians. The Phoenicians are condemned for disregarding the claims of brotherhood. Amos is moving to address the coastal region north of Israel where Tyre was their capital city.

'This is what Yahweh has said:
"For three transgressions by Tyre,
and especially for four, I will not reverse my decision.
Because they handed over an entire captivity to Edom,
and did not remember the covenant of brothers. (1:9)
So I will send fire against the wall of Tyre,
and it will consume its citadels."' (1:10)

The Phoenicians also were involved in slave-trading. The accusation is similar to the one aimed at the Philistines. Perhaps the Philistines were the raiders taking the captives, and the Phoenicians were the middlemen 'handing over' the slaves to those who wanted to buy them. Tyre was well-known for buying slaves (see Ezekiel 27:13) and selling them for a profit.

A particular evil was that the Phoenicians *'did not remember the covenant of brothers'*. Tyre had made a treaty with a nearby nation. There was a treaty between Solomon and Tyre many years before (see 1 Kings 5:12). A similar treaty had obviously been made with a nearby nation and so a 'brotherhood' had come into being between the two nations. But then Tyre betrayed all its promises and *'did not remember the covenant of brothers'*, actually invading the brother nation in order to sell captives into slavery.

1. **God is pleased when nations develop brotherly relationships**. The 'covenant of brothers' obviously was pleasing to God. Nations ought to be concerned about each other. Each country needs to look not only to its own interests but also to the interests and concerns of surrounding nations. It is good when nations become interdependent so that they are motivated to keep the peace internationally as well as within their own borders. International friendship between countries pleases God – as Amos lets us know. It is not that there is any kind of salvation in international peace. Far from it. The nations can be complacent and prosperous despite serious evils within their midst. But peace is worth seeking. It is not a way of salvation, but it is worth having nevertheless.

2. **God takes seriously the wickedness of betraying any kind of brotherly relationship**. Brotherly relationships within the

nations may be a fragile and feeble bond in an unsaved world, but Amos makes it clear that God looks for such brotherliness and is angered when it is ruptured by disloyalty and betrayal. The Phoenicians betrayed a country with whom they were in treaty-relationship. God will destroy Tyre as a result. *'So I will send fire against the wall of Tyre, and it will consume Tyre's citadels'*. The continuation of a society depends on God's will. Sin is likely to be punished by extermination. Tyre eventually ceased to exist. Tyre's fortified wall could not withstand the divine fire.

Chapter 14

Sins Against Humanity

(Amos 1:11–15)

Amos continues to look at the nations surrounding Israel, nations that the roaring lion is about to devour.

These sins that God denounces are all sins against humanity. And they are sins against conscience. Amos does not quote the Mosaic law until he begins to speak to Judah. He expects the pagan nations to know that these things are sins because they have a conscience. A sense of obligation to fellow human-beings is written into our very human nature.

The Edomites are condemned for stifling compassion. They had a persistently murderous spirit.

'This is what Yahweh has said:
"For three transgressions by Edom,
and especially for four, I will not reverse My decision.
Because he pursued his brother with the sword,
and he destroyed those to whom he should have shown mercy.
His anger raged perpetually,
and his rage persisted always."' (1:11)

Again Edom's sin was also a sin against brotherliness, but there were some other aspects to the matter.

1. **God looks for mercy in the human race**. It is part of human wickedness that men and women without God become unmerciful (Romans 1:31). The Medes had no mercy (Isaiah 13:18). Babylon had no mercy. 'You did not show mercy to my people' said God to Babylon (Isaiah 47:6). Especially God looks for us to show mercy to those to whom we are neighbours or have some kind of brotherly relationship.

Amos refers, it seems, to Edom's hostility to Israel. Edom pursued his brother Israel with the sword. Time and time again in Edom's history they showed bitterness and hostility towards Israel. Yet there was a special relationship between Edom and Israel. They were both descendants of Abraham.

2. **God hates anger that does not finish before the end of the day**. *'His anger raged perpetually'*, says Amos. One can understand how many centuries ago, Esau should have been violently angry with Jacob (Genesis 27:41). But Esau recovered from his anger (Genesis 33:4). Now centuries later the Edomites are still violently angry with the Israelites. Their anger was everlasting.

But God says *'Let not the sun go down upon your wrath . . .'*. Notice that it does not say 'Let not the sun come up upon your wrath . . .'. There are people who are angry when they go to bed at night but have forgotten their anger by the morning. Well, that's better than anger going on for ever. But actually Scripture says, *'Let not the sun go down upon your wrath . . .'*. It means: recover from your anger before you go to sleep. Close the dispute with a sweet word of friendship before you go to bed that night – if the other person allows it.

But judgement without mercy will be shown to the person who is not merciful. God says:

> *'"So I will send fire against Teman,*
> *and it will consume the citadels of Bozrah."'* (1:12)

Edom will face God's judgement. The fire of His punishment will fall upon the Edomite cities, Teman and Bozrah.

What made God angry with the Ammonites was their despising the weak. They are condemned for savage treatment of pregnant women.

> *'This is what Yahweh has said:*
> *"For three transgressions by the people of Ammon,*
> *and especially for four, I will not reverse my*
> *decision.*
> *Because they ripped open the pregnant women of*
> *Gilead,*
> *in order to enlarge their territory."'* (1:13)

The soldiers sent out by the Ammonite leaders were guilty of the most awful war crimes. They murdered pregnant women in the most terrible way. God has special mercy towards those who are in any way weak or needy. The orphan, the poor, the pregnant woman, the foreigner – God has special tenderness towards all of these people.

The reason why God gets so angry when people treat other people with such violence is because the human race is sacred! Men and women are made in the image of God! You cannot treat people as things, or as machines, or as statistics, or in the same way that you might treat an animal. There is something about the human race that makes it entirely different from any other section of God's creation. Only the human race is created in the image of God.

The cause of Ammon's violence towards another nation was that it was eager to enlarge its territory. This was a longstanding sin of Ammon. You get it as far back as the days of Jephthah when they invented some story to wage war on Israel even at that time (see Judges 11:13–14). Amos 1:13–14 refers to something later but it is still the same old territorial ambition that is showing itself. People get greedy for power, greedy for increased territory. *'Sheol and Abaddon are never satisfied, nor are a person's eyes'* (Proverbs 27:20). Like ancient Babylon, many empires have been greedy for increase of territory and power. *'He is as greedy as the grave'* (Habakkuk 2:5).

It is not only politicians and national leaders. Power and wealth tend to make you greedy for more power, more wealth. You never get to the point where you say 'I have enough'.

But God hates it and will judge it.

> *'"So I will send fire against the wall of Rabbah,*
> *and it will consume its citadels.*
> *There will be shouting on the day of battle,*
> *and a tempest in the day of the windstorm.* (1:14)
> *Their king will go into exile,*
> *he and his princes together."*
> *Yahweh has spoken!'* (1:15)

Rabbah was an Ammonite town. God says He will destroy it. In some kind of military conflict, victory will be given to Ammon's enemies. The king of the nation will be removed, he and his fellow statesmen together. God has determined it will happen. His word shall – says Amos – certainly come to pass.

Of course all of these predictions came to pass. None of the nations that Amos mentions exists today – although Israel exists today! God wiped out of existence Edom and Ammon. A nation that gets too ambitious will be humbled in due course. Anyone who speaks of an empire upon which the sun will never set, will find the sun setting quite rapidly!

Chapter 15

The Centrality of God's Word

(Amos 2:1–5)

The people of Moab were condemned for maintaining resentment. They held on to animosity when the cause of that animosity had ceased. Amos is not only concerned with sins against Israel. The sin of Moab was a sin against Edom – who themselves are mentioned in 1:11–12 as a sinful nation.

'This is what Yahweh has said:
"For three transgressions by Moab,
and especially for four, I will not reverse My decision.
Because he burned the bones of the king of Edom to ashes."' (2:1)

The Moabites went to the tomb of a dead king, a king of Edom whom they hated. They took out the dead king's body and publicly burned his bones to ashes.

1. **God hates vindictiveness about the past**. There must have been many sins that were being committed in the land of Moab but the one that God hated the most was being vindictive and hateful about an enemy who no longer could do anything worth worrying about. The king of Edom – whoever he might have been – was dead. He could trouble the Moabites no longer. But so much did the Moabite leader hate even the memory of this Edomite king, he and his people felt they had to publicly express their hatred and scorn towards their dead enemy. God hated it.

2. **Vindictiveness about the past is generally totally useless**. What could be more useless than digging up a corpse and burning its bones? It could not do the king any harm!

3. **Hate poisons the hater more than the hated**. Although such vengefulness could not do any harm to the king of

Edom, it did a lot of harm to the Moabites. Angry bitterness of this kind destroys our peace of mind, twists our judgement, and closes down the channels of God's blessing.

4. **Vindictiveness brings down God's anger**. God was so angry with such persistent and longlasting hatred that He decided it was time to act. Soon the land of Moab would be destroyed. Kerioth – a prominent Moabite city – would be destroyed.

> *' "So I will send fire against Moab,*
> *and it will consume the citadels of Kerioth.*
> *Moab will die amidst great tumult,*
> *amid war cries and the blast of a trumpet.* (2:2).
> *I will destroy the nation's ruler,*
> *and will kill all the nation's officials with him."*
> *Yahweh has spoken!'* (2:3)

Moab would cease to exist altogether. The king would soon die. The nation's officials would perish. God hated vindictiveness. We had best repudiate vengeance altogether.

Amos has now mentioned six countries and has denounced six sins: unjust violence, using people for profit, disregarding the claims of brotherhood, stifling compassion, despising the weak, maintaining everlasting resentment.

Now a seventh nation is addressed, but there comes a surprise. Amos has a word for Judah, part of the original 'holy nation' chosen by God.

> *'This is what Yahweh has said:*
> *"For three transgressions by Judah,*
> *and especially for four, I will not reverse my decision.*
> *Because they have rejected the law of Yahweh, and have not kept his statutes." '* (2:4)

What makes God angry with Judah is their despising His written word. We notice here a contrast in the way God spoke to the nations and the way God speaks to Judah. The six nations condemned in 1:3–2:3 were never condemned for disobeying God's law. They were never given God's law. The law of God was given exclusively to Israel on one definite occasion on Mount Sinai. No other nation was given a revelation of God's will in that way.

The nations mentioned in 1:3–2:3 were condemned for sinning against conscience. They knew – without possessing

God's law – that what they were doing was sin. But they did not have an additional revelation in written form. God never condemned them for breaking His law, since they did not possess His law. *'Everyone who has sinned without the law will also perish without the law; and everyone who has sinned, although he or she has the law, will be judged by the law'* (Romans 2:12). Every person is judged in terms of what they know.

But Judah had a written revelation of the will of God! They – unlike the surrounding nations – had *'rejected the law of Yahweh'* and had not *'kept his statutes'*. The law or (as the Hebrew word has it) 'Torah' of Yahweh is basically the written teaching we now have in our 'Pentateuch' – the first five books of our Bible. 'Rejecting the law' means idolatry and its social consequences, doing the kind of things we have mentioned in Amos 5: despising the courts (5:10, 15), trampling on the poor (5:11), oppressing the righteous (5:12), taking bribes (5:12), rejecting the prophets' call to heed the law of Moses.

Amos continues:

' "Their lies have led them astray,
their lies after which their fathers walked." ' (2:4)

'Their lies' refers to their self-deceit in failing to heed God's Word. It will refer also to heeding false prophecies – which tend to come in once the written revelation of God is neglected. It is a continuing problem among the people of God and is found today as much as it was to be found in Amos' day. Israel's ancestors tended always to neglect or misuse God's written Word – and so do we Christians today. We are still 'walking in the ways of our fathers'.

'Their lies have led them astray'. If we neglect God's written word it will lead us astray in our minds. We shall accept false teaching. It will lead us astray in our experience. We shall experience darkness and failure rather than life and illumination and the joy of God's presence. If we neglect God's written word, we shall be led astray in our behaviour. The church is ruined when it neglects God's written word.

God's says:

' "So I will send fire upon Judah,
and it will devour the strongholds of Jerusalem." ' (2:5)

To neglect God's written revelation always brings ruination.

Chapter 16

Grace and Ingratitude

(Amos 2:6–9)

Now after speaking to seven nations, Amos reaches the eighth: Israel. He began his survey of the nations by talking of Israel's seven neighbours. Now he has completed the circle and he comes to Israel itself. Israel was no different from the others!

> *'This is what Yahweh has said:*
> *"For three transgressions by Israel,*
> *and especially for four, I will not reverse My decision.*
> *Because they sell the righteous for money,*
> *and they sell the poor for a pair of sandals.* (2:6)
> *They trample the head of the helpless into the dust of the ground*[1]
> *and they push the poor out of the way.*
> *Not only the son, but even the father goes after the servant-girl,*[2]
> *in order to desecrate My name* (2:7).
> *I will not reverse my decision, because they spread out beside every altar the garments taken as security for a loan.*
> *In the house of their God they drink the wine taken as a fine."'* (2:8)

It is clear from the book of Amos that land was taken from the poor, then clothing, and that finally the poor fell into slavery because of their debts. When the poor tried to get justice in the law-courts they were pushed aside and judges were bribed. The Mosaic law defended the poor and needy in various ways, but at this time in Israel's history wealthy people within Israel had enough power to bribe the judges.

Many sins are mentioned here. (i) Selling the poor into

slavery (2:6b). The righteous person falls into debt. He owes a minutely small sum, the value of a pair of shoes. He cannot pay, and the man owed the sum sells him into slavery. (ii) Withholding justice from the poor (2:7a). *'They trample the head of the helpless into the dust of the ground'* refers to rough treatment in which the poor man is knocked to the ground by those who are rich, powerful and corrupt. *'They push the poor out of the way'* refers not only to ill-treatment but to the withholding of justice. As in 5:12 the poor person is pushed aside when he is on the way to a court seeking justice. (iii) Ill-treatment of servant-girls. *'Not only the son, but even the father goes after the servant-girl'*. It is not a reference to the same girl (the word 'same' does not occur in the Hebrew), but to the fact that both father and son are guilty of the same sin. They forced into immorality girls who could not easily resist the pressures of those who were powerful. (iv) Contempt for Yahweh. They followed their lusts knowing that what they were doing was offensive to God, They acted deliberately *'in order to desecrate'* God's revealed character as the holy God. (v) Depriving the poor of their last warm clothing. According to Exodus 22:26–27 when a poor person fell into extreme debt he would leave, during the daytime, his warm outer garment with the person owed the money. It was a sign of his indebtedness. But it was only a formality and the law demanded that the poor person should have his warm outer garment given back to him in the evening, It was illegal to keep the warm outer garment overnight. Yet the wealthy in Israel were taking the warm outer garments of the poor. (vi) Following a luxurious, lazy and sensuous lifestyle. They would spread out the blankets taken from the poor beside the altars where they went for their late-night parties at their idolatrous sanctuaries. The money they had taken from the poor in corrupt legal cases they then used to buy their wine, for their sessions of heavy drinking.

The terrible thing about all of this was that it was deep ingratitude. God had done so much for them. They had received a great salvation. Unlike the six nations of Amos 1:3–2:3 they had experienced at a national level God's redemption given to them by the blood of a lamb.

Amos 2:6–8 lists the sins of Israel. Amos 2:9–12 shows how

their sins are sins against grace, sins against the great things God has done for them. Amos 2:13–16 will go on to tell of how because of their wickedness God will bring a great tragedy into the life of Israel from which no one will escape.

What mighty things God had done for them! Amos refers to the time when God had brought them out of Egypt and into the land of Canaan. He has the whole nation (Judah and north Israel combined) in His mind.

> *'"Yet it was I who destroyed the Amorite before*
> *them,*
> *whose height was like the height of the cedar-tree,*
> *and who was as powerful as the oak trees.*
> *I destroyed his fruit from above,*
> *and his roots from beneath."'* (2:9)

'Amorite' is another word for 'Canaanite'; it refers to the original inhabitants of the land of Canaan (as in Genesis 15:16). God had enabled Israel to defeat all its enemies. As they had come into the land of Canaan, God had given them victory over Heshbon and Bashan, the first two Canaanite (or 'Amorite') nations which they met. Then God gave them victory over Jericho and the various fortresses of Canaan. The Israelites were simply a mob of ex-slaves, and the towns of Canaan were strong and powerful, *'like the height of the cedar-tree ... as powerful as the oak trees'*. But God gave them total and amazing victory and their Canaanite enemies were conquered thoroughly. God *'destroyed his fruit from above, and his roots from beneath'* until there was nothing left!

God wants us to be grateful for our redemption and to work out our redemption in the way in which we live. When the pagan world sins, it sins against conscience. When the people of God sin, they sin against grace. They sin against the great things God has done for them. Nothing could be more terrible. It is worse to sin against grace than to sin against conscience.

Footnotes

[1] I take it (i) that *hashsho'aphim* derives from *sh-'-ph*, 'to crush, trample', (ii) that 'head ...' is object of the verb, and (iii) that 'upon dust of the ground' is in Hebrew a locative phrase.

[2] The Hebrew word refers to a servant-girl and is never used (despite some expositions) of the temple-prostitute of pagan religion.

Chapter 17

Grace and Judgement

(Amos 2:10–16)

The terrible thing about Israel's wickedness was that they were sinning against God's mercy and grace. God had done so much for them, and they were sinning so unnecessarily. God had given them so much.

1. **They were sinning against previous victories**, as we have already seen. God had enabled Israel to defeat all their enemies (2:9).

But there is more.

'*"It was I who brought you up out of the land of Egypt,*
and I led you in the wilderness for forty years,
so that you could take possession of the land of the Amorite."' (2:10)

2. **They were sinning against redemption**. God had redeemed them out of bondage, released them from the oppression of Pharaoh and his officials, and had taken them out of the land they had lived in. He gave them a new life altogether. Yet now they had fallen into such awful sins.

3. **They were sinning against God's leading**. For forty years God had given them His guidance while they were in a dangerous wilderness. The pillar of fire and the pillar of smoke had led them step by step taking them to places where there was food or water.

4. **They were sinning against God's purpose for their lives**. God had a good purpose for them. He wanted them to take possession of the land of the Amorite, and be a light to the rest of the world by the way they lived in their new land. But in the way in which Israel was living they were far from being a light to lighten the Gentiles.

5. **They were sinning against God's word spoken and written.** Amos continues his list.

'"I raised up some of your sons to be prophets,
and some of your choice young men to be
Nazirites.
Is this not really the way it is, you people of Israel?"
It is an oracle of Yahweh!' (2:11)

God had sent prophets to the nation. Some of them, including Amos himself, would have their prophecies put into writing. The sins of Israel were sins against God's word, spoken and written.

6. **They were sinning against examples of godliness and discipline**. God had appointed some people to be 'Nazirites'. They were people who specially separated themselves from the ordinary affairs of life, so as to be able to give themselves specially to God's work. They abstained from drinking wine or intoxicating drinks. They avoided any kind of uncleanness. Some Nazirites were consecrated in this way for their whole lifetime. They provided an example for the rest of Israel of people who lived supremely for Yahweh.

But, says Amos, even these great gifts were despised and misused by the people of Israel.

'"But you made the Nazirites drink wine!
To the prophets you gave commands, saying,
'You shall not prophesy!'"' (2:12)

So now God announces His judgement against Israel just has He has done against the other nations.

'"So look! I am groaning beneath the burden you
are to me,
just as a cart that is fully loaded with sheaves
groans with the weight."' (2:13)

God can bear it no more. There have been 'three transgressions by Israel' and even more! God must now bring His judgement upon them, and there will be no escaping it.

'"Flight will fail the swift,
and the mighty will not prevail with his strength,
The warrior will not save his life. (2:14)
The archer will not stand his ground.
The fast runner will not save himself.
The charioteer will not save his life. (2:15)

Even the bravest among the warriors
will run away naked on that day."
Yahweh has spoken!' (2:16)

It is to be noticed that the punishment facing Judah and Israel is different from the punishment facing the six surrounding nations. The six nations of 1:3–2:3 will be exterminated; they will cease to exist. *'I will send fire against the house of Hazael, and it will consume the citadels ... I will cut off the sovereign ... it will consume its citadels ... the Philistines will perish even to the remnant ... I will send fire against the wall of Tyre ... it will consume its citadels ... I will send fire against Teman ... it will consume the citadels ... I will send fire against the wall of Rabbah ... it will consume its citadels ... I will send fire against Moab ... it will consume the citadels of Kerioth ... I will destroy the nation's ruler, and will kill all the nation's officials with him'* (1:4, 7, 8, 10, 12, 14; 2:2, 3).

All of this is the language of annihilation. There will be a total extinguishing of these nations so that they no longer exist on planet earth. Similar language is used of Judah. *'I will send fire upon Judah, and it will devour the strongholds of Jerusalem'*. At least temporarily the temple fortress at Jerusalem will be raised to the ground. Yet for Judah and Israel Amos will envisage some kind of survival, as we shall see. The six surrounding nations of 1:3–2:3 which have sinned against conscience – will be annihilated. The people of God will not.

Yet nothing will bring deliverance in that day when God acts against Israel. Speed will not help; flight will fail the swift. Mighty strength will be of no use. Powerful weapons will fail. Skill and techniques will do no good. The bravest of the brave will become cowards on the day God takes action.

God is still the Lord of the nations. He can still wipe a wicked nation out of existence any time He chooses. He can still send the severest calamities upon any people who disregard the privileges God has given to them. What can Christians do amidst the vast numbers of the nations? We can speak. We can train our children. We can pray. We can make it clear that we will not cooperate with the world's way of doing things. We can be involved in the society in which we live. It only takes a determined handful to swing the destiny of a nation. Meanwhile God judges the nations, often enduring 'three transgressions' but then there comes a time when His longsuffering comes to an end and He decides to act.

Chapter 18

A Last Opportunity

(Amos 3:1–8)

Amos 3:1–8 belongs with 1:2–2:16. This is clear for two reasons. (i) Amos ends with the same point with which he began. Yahweh has roared like a lion (1:2). *'A lion has roared. Who will not fear?'* (3:8). This is a common way of winding up a section of writing. You finish off confirming the point with which you started. (ii) A further reason is to be found in the content of 3:1–8. Amos is pressing upon his readers the message of what was said in chapters 1–2; so it belongs with what precedes, not with what follows.

1. **Being chosen by God has dangers to it**. Amos is now stressing the urgency of the matter.

> *'Hear this word which Yahweh has spoken against you, you people of Israel, against the family which I brought up from the land of Egypt:* (3:1)
> *"You only have I known of all the families of the earth. Therefore I will punish you for all your iniquities."'* (3:2)

Predestination is not favouritism! It is being chosen to be God's people. Israel was chosen uniquely, but this will mean that God will be all the more determined to get the nation to be the holy people of God.

2. **There is a covenant-relationship between God and Israel**. *'Will two walk together unless they have come to an agreement?'* (3:3). If two people are walking down the road together, then there has been some kind of arrangement between them. Either they had agreed to meet, or they met by accident and then agreed to walk together. God had 'met' Israel at Sinai and they had agreed to walk together.

3. **God's threats are aroused by human sinfulness**. There is a cause-and-effect relationship between sin and judgement. Amos has a string of questions which – except for 3:2 – come in pairs.

'Will a lion roar in a forest when there is no prey for him?' (3:4a). God is like a roaring lion! But there is a reason for it. He is not angry without a cause; God's anger is always a reaction to human sin. If God the lion is roaring, it is because sin is His prey. God's anger is not without cause. He takes no delight in His anger. The lion is roaring for one reason only.

'Will a lion growl in his den, unless he has caught something?' (3:4b). The picture moves on to a period a little while later. The lion is now in his lair growling contentedly over the prey which he has taken. It is important to notice that there is a time-gap between verse 3a and 3b. In verse 3a the lion is roaring but the prey is not taken yet. This is the way it was in 760 BC or thereabouts, 'two years before the earthquake' (1:1). The lion was roaring but there was still time for repentance. But in Amos 3:4b the situation has changed. The lion is now contentedly growling over its prey. *'For three transgressions ... and especially for four ...'*. After three transgressions the lion starts roaring. By the fourth transgression it is all over; the lion is feasting on the remains. But there was a time-gap between the roaring and the growling! God is roaring against sin; there is just a little time to escape – and then there will be nothing but the dead body.

4. **God gives a last warning.** *'For three transgressions ... and especially for four'*. Judah and Israel are getting very near 'the fourth transgression'. *'Will a bird fall into a trap on the ground when there is no bait for it?'* (3:5). The bird is fluttering around a deadly trap, but the trap could spring upon it at any moment. Again there is a time gap. The trap has not yet sprung. *'Will a trap spring up from the ground if it actually captures nothing?'* (3:5b). Maybe the bird will fly away! But God is giving a last warning. The bird is flying dangerously near the trap!

5. **God is in control of history and brings His judgements in His own time**. Amos is giving a last warning. *'If a trumpet is blown in a city, will the people not also be afraid?'* (3:6). Amos is like a man blowing a trumpet of warning. But again there is

a time gap between verse 6a and 6b. The calamities mentioned in Amos 1:3–2:16 have not happened yet. The trumpet blast is a last warning. Will be the people respond in fear and put right the wickedness of the nation? If not, soon calamity will fall. *'If there is calamity in a city, has Yahweh not done it?'* (3:6b). God will soon bring disaster upon the wicked nations. It will be His doing. The disasters that fall upon the nations are not accidents. God is in total control. God brings judgement at times when He sees judgement is appropriate. But there is a time gap! The calamity had not come at the point where Amos was preaching.

6. **The situation is now an open one – but it will soon close down.** God is announcing what will happen soon. *'Surely Yahweh does nothing unless He reveals his secrets to his servants the prophets'* (3:7). The people are getting a warning. God has given a predictive message to Amos. He has announced what is soon about to happen. 'A lion has roared. Who will not fear?' (3:8a). Because Amos knows he has been given a revelation and a call from Yahweh, he has no choice but to preach what he knows is God's word for the hour. 'Sovereign Yahweh has spoken. Who will not prophesy?' (3:8b).

At this point it is appropriate to go back to verse 3, and notice that it did not have a completion, as did the pairs in verses 4, 5 and 6.

Will two walk together unless they have come to an agreement? (3:3) – said Amos but then he stopped there. He could have added a second question, but in that verse he did not. It is a way of leaving the matter open. Israel and God were meant to be 'walking together'. An arrangement was made on Mount Sinai. God offered to make Israel a special treasure among all the peoples of the world (Exodus 19:5). But will Israel continue the arrangement. It has committed 'three transgressions' already. What will come next? Will the lion get its prey? Will the trap spring upon the fluttering bird? The situation will soon close down – in judgement or renewal. Which way will Israel follow?

Chapter 19

Useless Society; Useless Religion

(Amos 3:9–15)

Amos now starts a new section, which runs to Amos 6:14. Once again it is marked out by Amos' habit of beginning and ending a section with the same thought. He begins with a description of Samaria as a ruined and shattered kingdom (3:9–15), focusing on its powerlessness in holding on to what it has accumulated by violence (3:9–12), and on the uselessness of its religion (3:13–15). A dangerous enemy will soon surround the land. At the end of the section Amos returns to the same theme. God says He is 'raising up a nation' against Samaria (6:14) and He will devastate the land. Between those two points (3:9; 6:14) we have Amos' further analysis of Israel's corrupt society, produced by a corrupt religion. In 3:9–15 he has two accusations.

1. **Israel was full of chaos and violence**, and so God was raising up an enemy to destroy the land (3:9–12).

First, Amos invites two pagan peoples to witness what is happening in Israel: Ashdod, a Philistine town,[1] and Egypt. Two groups of people which were the traditional enemies of Israel are invited to see what is happening. The residents of the palaces of Philistia and Egypt are invited to judge the residents of the palaces in Samaria.

' "Cry out to the palaces in Ashdod,
and to the palaces in the land of Egypt.
Say to them, 'Gather yourselves on the hills of
Samaria,
and see the many uproars inside it,
and the oppressions in its midst.' " ' (3:9)

'Uproars' means tumult, agitation, instability in the nation. There is such wickedness in Israel that even pagan nations know enough of right and wrong to pronounce judgement upon Israel.

The violence in Israel has become so normal, that people hardly think there is anything wrong with it.

'"'For they have no knowledge of doing right,'
says Yahweh,
'These people who accumulate the rewards of
violence and robbery in their palaces.'"' (3:10)

They will be utterly overthrown.

'Therefore thus says the sovereign Yahweh:
"An enemy! An enemy surrounding the land.
And he shall pull down your strength from you,
and your palaces shall be plundered."' (3:11)

The enemy is Assyria. Actually about thirty years later an Assyrian king marched west, invaded the kingdom of Syria and brought Israel under its power. Israel tried to resist Assyrian power but did not succeed in doing so. In 723 BC Israel fell; the people were exiled and Israel as an distinct nation ceased to exist. They had been warned by Amos more than thirty years before.

To explain the cause of God's anger, Amos uses an illustration taken from the Mosaic law.

'Therefore thus says Yahweh:
"As a shepherd rescues from the mouth of a lion,
two legs, or a piece of an ear,
so shall the people of Israel be rescued,
those who dwell in Samaria,
leaving only the corner of a bed, and a piece[2] *of a*
couch."' (3:12)

Amos' point is based on the law of Exodus 22:10–13. When a sheep was attacked by a lion and killed, the evidence of the incident had to be produced, if the shepherd was not to be accused of theft. After the lion had done its work perhaps only a few scraps of the sheep were left but these had to be produced as evidence of what had happened.

When Assyria has done its work, Israel will be utterly devastated. Nothing will be left except a few scraps. Amos says what will be left will be *'the corner of a bed, and a piece of a couch'*! This will be all that will remain of Israel. As the few remaining scraps indicate what sort of animal was killed by the lion, the few remaining scraps of Israel will show what sort of nation it was: a nation whose remains are beds and couches! A nation that had got used to a lazy and sensuous lifestyle.

2. **Israel's religion was powerless to help**. The important question to ask about our faith is: does it deliver us from the degenerate ways of the world around us. In Israel it did not!

> *'"Hear and testify against the house of Jacob."*
> *Oracle of the sovereign Yahweh, the Almighty* (3:13)
> *"For on that day when I will punish the*
> *transgressions of Israel,*
> *I will also punish the altars of Bethel.*
> *And the horns of the altar shall be broken*
> *and shall fall to the ground.* (3:14)
> *I will strike the winter house and the summer house*
> *and the houses of ivory shall perish,*
> *and the great houses shall come to an end."*
> *Oracle of Yahweh.'* (3:15)

In 3:9–12 Amos was concerned about fortresses and the rewards of war. In 3:13–15 Amos is concerned about altars, and religious sanctuaries. Just as the palaces were doomed, so the religion of Samaria was doomed also.

It was a religion that did not get rid of 'transgressions' or 'rebellions'. True faith in the promises of God leads to submission to the ways of God. Fake religion does nothing about rebelliousness. It does not change the heart.

It was a religion that did not bring people to know God. 'Beth-el', which means 'house of God', was famous as the place where Jacob the ancestor of the nation had met with God. Now people admired Bethel, but they knew nothing of Jacob's God or Jacob's experience of knowing God. Bethel itself would come under judgement.

It was a religion that did not bring people into a life of discipline. As Amos 3:12 has suggested, the people lived a life of luxury. They had their summer houses and their winter houses. There is nothing wrong with wealth, but we have to ask questions about how it is used. The wealth of Israel was used to make the people lazy and indolent. They loved luxury but they did not love God. And at this point their religion did not help them. It left them unchanged.

Footnotes

[1] Possibly we should ready 'Assyria' here (as the Greek Old Testament has it) but in a difficult textual decision I prefer to give the Masoretic text the benefit of the doubt.

[2] The Hebrew word here is of unknown meaning. 'A piece' gets the idea but which piece is unknown.

Chapter 20

The Cows of Bashan

(Amos 4:1–5)

Amos 3:9–4:5 is presenting Amos' analysis of Israel:

- the nation was full of violence (3:9–12);
- its religion was powerless (3:13–15);
- its upper-class citizens were arrogant (4:1–3);
- its pilgrimages were useless (4:4–5).

We can see that Amos mixes his criticism of society (3:9–12; 4:1–3) with his criticism of the nation's religion (3:13–15; 4:4–5).

1. **Israel's leading citizens were lazy and arrogant**. Amos has a special word for them. Many scholars take 4:1–3 to be an attack on upper-class women in Israel, but actually that interpretation is quite doubtful. Many of the Hebrew pronouns in this section are masculine plural in form ('Hear this', 'their' lords; the days are coming upon 'you'). It is not likely that women would be addressed with Hebrew masculine plurals. The 'cow' is a feminine word and this is enough to explain for some feminine pronouns in the Hebrew. But it is more difficult to explain why women should be spoken of with masculine plural pronouns. Admittedly, the use of a masculine for a feminine can be found in Hebrew, but a mixture of masculine and feminine forms needs more precise explanation. The picture is best taken as a metaphor in which men who think they are brave and bold in their sins are ridiculed by the prophet as being like animals. The Hebrew pronouns make it difficult to think that women are being specially addressed.

> *'Hear* [masc.] *this word, you cows* [fem.] *of Bashan*
> *who live in the highlands of Samaria,*

cows who [fem.] *oppress the poor and crush the needy,*
cows who [fem.] *say to their* [masc.] *lord,*[1]
"Bring in provisions that we may drink!"' (4:1)

The drinking-sessions took place in the sanctuaries of the pagan gods. The leaders of Samaria are like animals, living only for physical comfort and bodily pleasures. They care nothing of how others in their own land are suffering. The poor have to suffer in order that the rich may have their physical comforts.

These upper-class leaders of the land rather liked the degenerate religion of Israel; they liked the idea of a god who provided for all their greeds!

Like animals they live; and like cows – says Amos – they will be led away with hooks in their noses!

'My sovereign Yahweh has sworn by His holiness,
"Behold, the days are coming upon you [masc.],
when they will take you [masc.] *away with meat hooks,*
and your [fem.] *rear guard with fishhooks.* (4:2)
Through the breaches in the walls you [fem.] *will go out,*
Each one [fem.] *straight before her* [fem.].
And you [fem.] *will be sent beyond Harmon."'* (4:3)

'Harmon' is the name of an unknown town, somewhere beyond Damascus. We must notice the reference to the oath of God. *'My sovereign Yahweh has sworn by his holiness'*. When God takes an oath, it means that a decision has been made, and it will not be able to be changed.

2. **Again Amos turns from social matters to religious matter**. The pilgrimages of the people were useless. It is obvious that the people of Amos's day loved visiting the famous sanctuaries at Bethel and Gilgal, just as today people might like to visit Mecca or Jerusalem or Canterbury Cathedral (in Britain).

'"Come to Bethel – and sin!
Come to Gilgal – and rebel! Rebel repeatedly!
Bring your sacrifices for the morning,
your tithes every three days. (4:4)
Burn thanksgiving-offerings with leaven!"' (4:5)

We remember that the law forbade sacrifices with leaven (Exodus 34:25; Leviticus 2:11).

> *'"Proclaim freewill offerings!*
> *Announce them well!*
> *For that is what you love, you people of Israel."*
> *Oracle of my sovereign Yahweh!'* (4:5)

Bethel and Gilgal were famous for two events in the story of Israel. Bethel was the place where Jacob – the ancestor of Israel – first met with God. He was running away from a situation where he had brought much trouble upon himself, and suddenly God stepped into his life. Then, again, later in his life Jacob was taken back to Bethel, the place where he had met God. After many trials in his life God took him again to Bethel, and he was asked to build an altar there (Genesis 35:1). Bethel was a reminder of the possibility of meeting with God. But later in Israel's history, Jeroboam I built an idolatrous shrine there and it became the place of wickedness.

The people loved going to Bethel, but they were not meeting with the God of Bethel, the God who disturbs those who are fugitives from righteousness, the God who turns their lives around.

Gilgal was famous too. It was the place where there was a monument commemorating the crossing of the river Jordan (Joshua 4:19–24). God did amazing things in bringing Israel to the land of Canaan. Idols are dead but the God of the Bible is the living God! Joshua wanted people to remember their spiritual history, so he built a pile of stones at Gilgal to remind the people of what God had done. A nation came into being because *'the hand of the Lord is mighty'* (Joshua 4:24). Joshua said, *'I am doing this so that you may fear Yahweh your God for ever'* (Joshua 4:24). Gilgal was the place where the Israelites were first circumcised after coming into the land of Canaan.

But now in Amos' day the people go to Gilgal on pilgrimage but they forget that 'The hand of Yahweh is mighty'. They go to Gilgal on pilgrimage but they forget that Gilgal was a place where the male Israelites symbolized their dedication and purity for God.

The people went to Bethel but did not meet God. They went to Gilgal but did not purify their hearts. They had plenty of religion – especially freewill offerings – but their religion did not involve contact with the living God because it was displeasing to Him.

What does God want of us? First a meeting with Him in faith. Trust in Jesus. He wants us to be like Jacob and say 'The God of the Bible will be my God'. Then He wants dedication, discipline, social concern, righteousness. People love religion; but the same people do not always love righteousness.

Footnote

[1] The Hebrew for 'their lord' is not the common word for husband. 'Their lord' seems to refer to a god. Like the Hebrew word for 'God' it is plural in form but singular in meaning. The phrase is similar to 'their god' in 2:8.

Chapter 21

Preparing to Meet God

(Amos 4:6–13)

Amos has analysed the state of Israel's society (3:9–4:3). Now he makes the point that this social and religious rebellion has continued despite the chastening of God.

1. **God is able to severely chasten His church**. Israel was the equivalent of the church. It was a nation-church, a church and a nation at the same time. It was not, of course, the post-Pentecost church, yet it was the spiritual 'people of Abraham' in the form of a nation. True believers were almost entirely within Israel. Israel was a shadow of the church. It was the form that was taken by the people of God before the fuller coming of the Holy Spirit.

We must apply the lessons that Amos taught Israel to ourselves. God was able to severely chasten Israel; and He is able to severely chasten His church. Churches in one part of the world or another might go through a period of severe discipline. Those who attack God's word or resist the moving of the Spirit may find that an atmosphere of death settles upon the churches in that area. The expansion of the church in one part of the world might totally by-pass those elsewhere who are experiencing severe chastening.

God severely chastened Israel but it did no good, since the nation did not respond.

God brought famine.

' "I brought famine in every city,
and lack of bread in every town –
but you have not returned to Me."
Oracle of Yahweh.' (4:6)

God brought drought.

'"I also withheld rain from you, three months
before the harvest.
I sent rain on one town, but withheld it from
another.
One field had rain; another had none and dried
up. (4:7)
People from two or three cities stumbled to
another city to drink water,
but did not have their thirst quenched.
But you have not returned to Me."
Oracle of Yahweh.' (4:8)

God brought damage to the crops.

'"I repeatedly sent a scorching wind and brought
damage to the crops;
the locust devoured your gardens and your
vineyards, your fig trees and your olive trees.
But you have not returned to me."
Oracle of Yahweh.' (4:9)

God brought plague and defeat.

'"I sent a plague on you like the one I sent on
Egypt.
I killed your young men with the sword,
I took your horsemen away.
And I made the smell of dead bodies arise in your
camps.
But you have not returned to me."
Oracle of Yahweh.' (4:10)

God brought destruction.

'"I destroyed some of you,
as God destroyed Sodom and Gomorrah,
and you were truly a scorched stick saved from the
fire.
But you have not returned to me."
Oracle of Yahweh.' (4:11)

2. **God goes on offering a way back to Him until the very last moment**. Once He 'takes an oath' and decides to act, nothing can stop what He intends to do. But before He finally takes action, He may give one last warning, and this is what we find in Amos 4:12–13.

'"So then, this is what I have been doing to you.
And because I have been doing this to you,
you are to prepare to meet your God, O Israel."' (4:12)

God gives Israel a final offer. The words *'Prepare to meet your God'* are surely an offer of grace, not a threat of doom. There are three reasons for saying this.

(i) The idea of 'meeting God' may refer to experiencing His grace, as well as facing His punishment. *'Moses brought out the people ... to meet God'*, says Exodus 19:17, but it is not referring to punishment.

(ii) The very fact that God is still speaking to Israel through Amos means that God is still wanting to send last-minute blessing to Israel. If God were planning only final judgement, God would not be still speaking to Israel. While God is speaking to us, final judgement has not yet come. Today if we hear His voice, we can respond to Him, for He is still speaking to us.

(iii) It is also important to note that the Hebrew of Amos 4:13 can speak of God 'who makes the dawn out of darkness'. It does not necessarily mean 'who makes darkness out of dawn' – and that is the less likely translation. It more likely speaks of hope than of doom. The power of God to create is an encouragement! So we have here a last offer. God has been chastising the people. Now He says 'Because I have been doing this to you, you are to prepare to meet your God'. The chastening is a sign that God is still wanting to work in Israel's life.

Verse 13 is a quotation from a song, maybe written by Amos, maybe quoted by Amos from someone else.

'For behold!
The Shaper of the mountains,
and the Creator of the wind,
the One who declared his secrets to Adam,
the One who makes dawn out of darkness,
the One who treads upon the mountains of earth –
Yahweh, the Almighty God is his name.' (4:13)

It is a song about God's power to create (*'Shaper of the mountains ... Creator of the wind'*), and God's power to give fresh understanding (*'One who declared his secrets to Adam'*). We remember that after God had created the universe, and humankind as the climax of creation, then God had fellowship with Adam, as Genesis 3:8 suggests.

Amos's song goes on to speak of God as the One who can change the darkest and gloomiest situation (*'the One who makes dawn out of darkness'*), the One who can move the most immovable obstacle (*'the One who treads upon the mountains of earth'*). His name reveals him to be the God who redeems by blood, the Redeemer-God of the Exodus ('Yahweh') and the One who contains all powers within Himself ('Almighty God' means 'the God who is hosts'; He contains 'hosts' of powers within Himself).

All of this is said to encourage Israel to come back to God. If God can recreate and reveal His plans, if He can change the darkest situation – why should Israel not come back to Him?

Chapter 22

Death or Life

(Amos 5:1–5)

The trend of thought in this section of Amos goes like this. Amos says that there is an enemy encircling the land of Israel. It is about to invade and destroy at any moment. The cause of the invasion is the sin of Israel.

Amos has given a general sketch of Israel's spiritual lunacy (3:9–4:3):

- failure in the palaces of Samaria (3:9–12)
- powerless religion (3:13–15)
- arrogant leadership (4:1–3)
- useless pilgrimages (4:4–5).

And he has spoken of the failure of God's chastisements (4:6–13):

- famine (4:6)
- drought (4:7–8)
- ruin of crops (4:9)
- pestilence (4:10)
- earthquake (4:11)
- a last invitation (4:12–13).

Many calls from God have gone unheeded (4:6–11). God is giving Israel a last call to repentance (4:12–13).

Now Amos sings a song over Israel, and the song is a 'lamentation', a 'funeral song'. He says: *'Hear this word which I take up over you in lamentation, O house of Israel'* (5:1). 'Listen to this funeral-song which I am going to sing'.

The theme of the section is: Seek God or die as a nation. Heed God's last call or perish. (Actually Israel did 'perish' and die as a nation less than forty years after Amos' ministry. The Assyrians invaded Israel in the late 720s BC, and northern Israel, with its capital-city Samaria, was destroyed.) The death song is to be found in 5:1–3 and continues in 5:16–17. Seeking God is mentioned in 5:4–5 and 5:14–15. The sins of Israel are explained in 5:7 and 5:10–13. In the heart of the section is a song about the great power of God (5:8–9). This means that the sections of the poetry have an A-B-C-D-C-B-A structure.

A. The death-song (5:1–3)
  B. Seeking God but not at the sanctuaries (5:4–5)
    C. You ... turn justice into bitterness (5:7)
      D. He ... The God who makes changes (5:8–9)
    C. You ... turn righteousness to bribery (5:10–13)
  B. Seeking God (5:14–15)
A. The death-song (5:16–17)

Amos sings a funeral son (5:1–3). It is the kind of song you might sing when someone has died.

'The virgin Israel has fallen;
she will never stand up again;
she has been left lying on her land;
no one raises her up.' (5:2)

The Assyrians have not come yet but Amos is already singing the funeral-song! Israel is about to face destruction in a way that is so terrible the nation will go out of existence, and will never be raised up again in the same form as she was in before.

The cause of the destruction will be military invasion.

'For thus says my Lord Yahweh:
"The city that went out a thousand strong
shall have only a hundred left;
and the one that went out a hundred strong
shall have only ten left –
O house of Israel."' (5:3)

The only hope for Israel is to seek God – but not at the idolatrous sanctuaries (5:4–5).

'For thus says Yahweh,
"O house of Israel:
Seek Me and live! (5:4).
But do not seek Me at Bethel,
and do not come to Gilgal,
and do not cross over to Beersheba.
Because Gilgal will certainly go into exile,
and Bethel will become nothing."' (5:5)

Bethel, Gilgal and Beersheba were three famous places in Israel's history, but in Amos' time they had become places of idolatry. All three of them were famous as places where God gave newness of life to His people. Bethel was famous as the place where meeting God changed Jacob's life. Gilgal was famous as the place where Israel crossed the Jordan and started a new life in Israel. Beersheba was famous as the place where God told Abraham, Isaac and Jacob that He would be with them. Amos was singing a song about death. The people were making pilgrimages to shrines which earlier in Israel's history spoke about life! Life or death? Which way would Israel go? God was giving them a last warning. The sin of Israel was bringing about its death. The wages of sin is death. The soul that sins shall die. 'Death' in Hebrew thinking is something progressive. Every sin is a fatal blow. Those who sow to the flesh reap corruption, because every wickedness corrupts and destroys. Only those who do the will of God abide.

1. **Bethel was famous as a life-changing place**. Jacob (see Genesis 28:10–22) was running away from home because his sins had got him into trouble. There God spoke to him. There the angels came down upon him. And a few years later (see Genesis 35:1–15) in the same place, he became a new man and was given the name Israel.

But now in Amos's time Bethel was a place of spiritual death. The life-giving God was no longer to be found there. It was a place of sin and wickedness. It did not impart any newness of life.

2. **Gilgal was famous as a place of renewal and purification.** God had done great things for them. A memorial was built there reminding them that *'the hand of the Lord is mighty'* (Joshua 4:1–24). There the passover was celebrated and the men were circumcised. It all spoke of newness of life, redemption by the blood of the lamb, consecration to God.

But now in Amos's time Gilgal was no longer reminding anyone that *'the hand of Yahweh is mighty'* (contrast Joshua 4:24). Seek God, says Amos, but don't go on pilgrimage to Gilgal. It is now a place of death, not a place of life.

3. **Beersheba was famous as the place where God spoke of His companionship with His people**. Abraham built altars at

Shechem and Bethel and Hebron, but it was at Beersheba that it became obvious God was planning to bless Abraham with newness of life. It was there that a pagan king could see that God was with Abraham and said to him *'God is with you'* (Genesis 21:23). It was there that God said to Isaac *'I am with you'* (Genesis 26:24). It was there that God said to Jacob *'I will go with you'* (Genesis 46:1, 4).

But the famous sanctuaries were useless; it was necessary to seek God afresh. 'Seek God', says Amos, but don't go the sanctuaries that have died. Seek God afresh!

Chapter 23

Making a Change

(Amos 5:6–13)

Amos is singing Israel's funeral-song already (5:1–5). 'Seek Yahweh', he says, but whatever you do don't go to the sanctuaries at Bethel, Gilgal and Beersheba (5:4–5). Bethel, Gilgal and Beersheba were famous for bringing great changes into the life of Abraham, Isaac and Jacob. God is a God of new birth, of newness of life. He is the God who brings about mighty changes in the lives of men and women. At Bethel, Jacob's name was changed to Israel. The change of name represented the newness of life God was giving to Jacob. But men and women tend to reverse God's changes and go back into the pathways of sin.

Turning one thing into another is the theme of the three inner units of Amos 5:1–16. Amos 5:6–7 is about making a change: 'You . . . turn justice into bitterness'. The song to God in Amos 5:8–9 is about the ability of God to make great changes. And Amos 5:10–13 spells out in detail how men and women change God-given righteousness into corruption of one kind or another.

1. **You turn justice into bitterness** (5:7). The people loved the national traditions of Israel, and were delighted when they could visit the famous worship-centres at Bethel. But Amos says, 'Don't just follow dead and corrupted traditional religion. Seek Yahweh himself'.

' "Seek Yahweh that you may live!
Otherwise He will break out like a fire, O house of Joseph,
and devour with nothing to quench it in Bethel. (5:6)

*You who turn justice into the bitter wormwood-
plant,
and who throw down righteousness to the
ground."'* (5:7)

Bethel was the place that was famous for bringing an immense change into the life of Jacob. Now the people of Israel are visiting the famous worship-centre, but they are reversing the very change that God brought into the life of Jacob. Jacob was changed from a man of deceit into a man of godliness and integrity. Now the people were admiring their national ancestor, and visiting the memorial of life at Bethel – but were not interested in having the same experience he had. Indeed they were undoing and reversing the very thing that had happened to Jacob. Unless they seek God Himself, He will exterminate northern Israel, as He did the pagan nations (note the similarity of 5:6 with 1:4, 7, 10, 12, 14; 2:2). There will be an annihilating, unquenchable fire if they do not repent.

They have turned the righteousness that God brought into Israel into *'the bitter wormwood-plant'* – a plant with a bitter and horrible taste. They have 'thrown down righteousness to the ground', disregarding justice and despising its claims.

2. **God turns night into day** (5:8–9). Amos inserts a song. It is a few lines from a hymn celebrating God as the one who brings about great changes.

*'"The One who one made the Pleiades and Orion,
and changes deep darkness into daylight,
who darkens the day into night;
the One who calls into being the waters of the sea,
and pours them out on the surface of the earth.
Yahweh is His name!* (5:8)
*The One who causes destruction to burst upon the
strong,
so that destruction comes upon the fortress."'* (5:9)

He changes the seasons of the year. 'Pleiades and Orion' are the names of groups of stars. They would be in different parts of the sky at different seasons of the year.

He makes changes day by day, turning night into daytime and daytime into night.

He makes the changes necessary for the weather to do His will. He created the seas and waters of the earth in the first place, and now controls them so that they do His will. He *'calls into being the waters of the sea, and pours them out on the surface of the earth'*.

He makes the changes involved in the salvation of men and women. *'Yahweh is His name!'* says Amos' song, reminding us that the Creator-God is also the Redeemer-God who 'got Himself a name' when He saved Israel by the blood of a lamb.

He makes the changes involved in the judgements of history when nations rise and fall, at the word of God's power. He can take mighty warriors and bring instant destruction upon them. He *'causes destruction to burst upon the strong'*. Fortresses are nothing to Him.

Each line of Amos' song makes the point that the God of Israel is the God who brings about massive changes with the greatest of ease, whenever He wishes. The pilgrims come to Bethel, allegedly admiring a God who mightily changed Jacob's life. They sing songs celebrating God's power to bring about changes in history, in nature, and in His relationships with men and women. And then they go away unchanged themselves. The only change they make is to turn justice into the wormwood-plant!

3. **You turn righteousness to bribery** (5:10–13). Proceeding back along the same line of thought, Amos lists the characteristics of the unchanged life.

'"They hate the one who reproves the wicked in
the gate,
and the one who speaks the truth. (5:10)
Therefore, because you trample upon the needy,
and extract levies of grain from them.
You built houses of hewn stone,
you will not live in them.
The pleasant vineyards that you planted,
you shall not drink their wine. (5:11)
I know that your transgressions are many,
and your sins are numerous,
you who distress the upright, and accept bribes,
and turn aside the poor from the gate. (5:12)
Therefore at such a time the wise person keeps
quiet,
for it is an evil time."' (5:13)

'The gate' was the gate of the city, the place where justice was administered. The people who loved to visit Bethel, hated a just judge (*'one who reproves the wicked'*) and the truthful witness (*'the one who speaks the truth'*). They were ill-treating the needy, and giving themselves to the life of luxury. They disregarded God's estimate of their sins (*'your transgressions are many . . . your sins are numerous'*). They allowed money to twist justice. They made life difficult for the honest person (*'the wise person keeps quiet'*).

But soon exterminating judgement will come. Their luxurious homes will not be lived in. No one will be around to enjoy the wine of the vineyards. The Assyrians will come; northern Israel will cease to exist – unless they turn to the God who changed Jacob at Bethel and still 'changes deep darkness into daylight'. Seeking God is their only hope.

Chapter 24

Seeking God

(Amos 5:14–20)

Amos comes back to the alternatives: seeking God (5:14–15) or hearing the funeral-song (5:16–17).

' "Seek good and not evil, in order that you may live,
and so that Yahweh, God Almighty,
will be with you, as you say. (5:14)
Hate evil; and love what is good,
and establish righteousness in the gate.
Perhaps Yahweh, God Almighty, will be gracious
to a remnant of Joseph." ' (5:15)

The alternative is to continue the funeral song. Amos returns in 5:16–17 to where he started in 5:1–5.

The key idea here is 'seeking'. It implies that at the moment in Israel's history, God is not immediately to be found. Experiencing His blessing will require 'seeking' – taking time and effort to request God to come back into the life of the nation. *'Seek me'*, said God (Amos 5:4). *'Seek Yahweh'* said Amos 5:6. *'Seek the good'* or *'Seek the Good One'* says Amos 5:14. *'It is time to seek Yahweh'* said Amos' contemporary Hosea (Hosea 10:12).

What is involved in seeking God? (i) It means that we give God time. We do not let the pressure of life be so great that we take God for granted and rush into everything else that interests us without considering God. (ii) It means that we talk to God. *'Take with you words'*, said Hosea 14:2. We ask His forgiveness. We admit what has happened in the life of the nation. (iii) It means that we turn away from the kind of life God hates; and we start living the kind of life that God approves of. *'Hate evil'* says God, through Amos. It requires a passionate resistance to everything we know is wicked. *'Love what is good'*; it requires an aggressive and determined commitment to what we know God likes. *'Establish righteousness in the gate'* says Amos. The 'gate' is the town gate where courts met for decisions on controversies. When righteousness is established in the law-courts and the poor can get justice, God will be pleased.

What will happen if they seek God in this way is that the life of the nation will be restored. *'Seek good ... in order that you may live'*, says God. Newness of life will flow into the people of God, if they establish justice for the needy people of the land.

It is almost too late. God is just about to exterminate the nation. The funeral song has commenced. But a last-minute repentance might bring last-minute rescue. 'Perhaps Yahweh, God Almighty, will be gracious to a remnant of Joseph'. Maybe a small section of the nation will be allowed to survive if they seek Yahweh now before it is too late. Otherwise the funeral song must continue.

> *'Therefore, this is what Yahweh, God Almighty, the sovereign, says:*
> *"In all the streets there will be lamentation,*
> *in the squares they will be saying, 'Alas! Alas!'*
> *They will summon the farm-workers to mourning*
> *and the professional mourners to wailing.* (5:16)
> *And in all the vineyards there will be lamentation,*
> *for I will pass through in the midst of you."*
> *Yahweh has spoken.'* (5:17)

If Israel will not seek God, soon the nation will be exterminated. In the streets and squares of the towns there will be distress. And in the rural areas also people will turn to mourning. When God comes in judgement – in the form of Assyrian invasion – it will be a funeral, and Israel will be found no more. Seeking God is the only hope. The alternative is extermination.

Amos seems to like the style in which one moves through topics to a central point and then works backwards through the same topics in reverse order. He does it again in Amos 5:18–27:

A. Inescapable judgement in the day of Yahweh (5:18–20)
B. Rejection of worship: festivals, offerings and singing (5:21–23)
C. Let justice rule (5:24)
B. Rejection of idolatry (5:25–26)
A. Inescapable exile (5:27)

Amos says:

'Woe to you who long for the Day of Yahweh!
What will that day be for you?
It will be darkness rather than light. (5:18)
It will be as if a man were escaping from a lion,
and a bear meets him.
Then he goes home and rests his hand on a wall,
and a snake bites him. (5:19)
Will not the day of Yahweh be darkness rather than light,
deep darkness with no brightness in it?' (5:20)

Amos has spoken to the people of the coming anger of God which will exterminate the land. But actually the people were a very religious people, and even a very theological people. They loved discussing the Day of the Lord. The coming of God was a most interesting teaching! When the people gathered in their great meeting-places at Bethel and Gilgal and Beersheba, the 'Day of Yahweh' was a favourite topic for discussion! It was so interesting!

People are the same today. Teaching about prophecy and 'the end-times' rouses a lot of interest. How people love to discuss the millennium, and the 'last days'. What excitement is generated when some prophet stands up to tell us what is about to happen in Israel, or how Armageddon is getting close. How eagerly placards and texts about 'the rapture' are bought in the Christian bookshops! But Amos has to ask the nation, 'What will that day be for you?' Only for those living for the approval of God will that day be a blessing. Soon 'the Day of the Lord' will come near to Israel. Assyrian invasion will be a foretaste of the end of the world. Yet for most of Israel it will be a day of inescapable judgement – like a man escaping from a lion. He runs for his life but when he turns a corner he meets a bear! He dashes away in another direction, and finally gets home. But when he rests his hand on a wall, a snake bites him. Inescapable punishment. If it does not come in one form it will come in another. For all who are not living for God – no matter how religious they are – the day of Yahweh will be darkness rather than light.

Chapter 25

Justice Flowing Like a River

(5:21–27)

The people of northern Israel loved their religion but it did them no good.

1. **God despises useless religion**. They liked the meetings, the sacrifices and the singing. Their 'worship' imitated the worship at Jerusalem, but it was corrupt and idolatrous. God says:

> '"*I hate, I detest your festivals,*
> *I do not take any delight in your solemn assemblies.* (5:21)
> *When you bring me burnt offerings and cereal offerings*
> *I will not accept them.*
> *And I will not take notice of*
> *the peace offerings of your fattened animals.* (5:22)
> *Take away from me the noise of your songs.*
> *I will not listen to the melody of your harps.*"' (5:23)

Festivals, sacrifices and musical worship were all involved in the worship of northern Israel but God hated all of it! The 'burnt offerings' symbolising consecration, the cereal offerings symbolising dedication of one's work to God, the peace offerings which spoke of the joys of reconciliation with God – all of them were disgusting to God. What was wrong with such 'worship'? It was offered to perverted 'gods' who were not the Redeemer-God of burning holiness. And it was a religion that ignored God's demand for justice, preferring self-centred pietism.

2. **God will accept only a faith that leads to abundant righteousness**. Religious routines that produce no abundance

of righteousness are abominations to God, however lively and interesting they might be. Amos says:

> *'"But let righteousness roll down like a flood of waters,*
> *let justice flow like a river that never stops flowing."'* (5:24)

Amos is specially thinking of the protection of the weak and poor, and the preservation of honesty in the law courts. God is looking for righteousness and justice.

It is interesting that Amos says *'Let righteousness roll down like a flood of waters . . . '*. It is the Hebrew word *galal*. It is closely linked to the name of the town Gilgal. 'I have rolled away the reproach of Egypt from you', said God, back in the days when the people of God were circumcised at Gilgal after coming to the promised land (Joshua 5:9). The disgrace of being displeasing to God had been 'rolled away', so the place became known as Gilgal – 'Rolling' (Joshua 5:9b). Now in Amos's time the people love to visit Gilgal, as a famous religious centre, but there is no 'rolling away' of the reproach of sin. Amos says *'Let righteousness roll down . . . '*.

3. **God despises religion invented by human preference**. Amos comes back to God's rejection of their religion. Amos 5:25–26 corresponds to 5:21–23.

'Was it sacrifices and offerings that you brought to Me during the forty years in the wilderness, O house of Israel?' (5:25). Of course Israel did bring sacrifices and offerings to God during the forty years in the wilderness! Exodus 18:12 refers to sacrifices brought by Jethro. Exodus 24:4, 6 shows us how Moses offered sacrifices in the wilderness. Leviticus 9:8–24 refers to sacrifices administered by Aaron. Numbers 7:19 tells us of offerings given to God in the wilderness period. The Passover was an obligatory sacrifice in the nation's life from the very day they first were redeemed from Egypt.

Amos's question means: is this all it was? Was it sacrifices and offerings that you brought to Me – and nothing more than that? Religious ritual that has no effect on one's attitude to the needy? And perhaps Amos's words also mean: Was it **these** sacrifices and offerings that you brought Me? Because verse 26 moves from the wilderness period to Amos' own time. *'You have carried around Sakkuth*[1] *your king* [an

Assyrian god], *and Kaiwan*[2] *your divine star* [the planet Saturn] – *these images of yours!'* (5:26). Was this what God ordained on Sinai?

It was the custom in the ancient world to carry around man-made 'gods', especially in religious ceremonies and in battles with other nations. The gods that Israel were now worshipping had little resemblance to Yahweh, the God who had saved the nation in the days of Moses, by the blood of the passover lamb. But they did not think that different ideas about God mattered very much! They had recently got their religious ideas from Assyria and Babylon! They now used the word 'Yahweh' in their 'new theology' from abroad! Their enthusiasm for their own revised edition of Israel's religion did not affect their attitudes to the poor, but that did not worry them.

Amos's preaching was entirely different. Amos knew Yahweh – the Redeemer God of Israel – as the God of holiness and righteousness. The people of Israel were careless about justice in society. They worshipped immoral gods. Amos holds to faith in the God who revealed Himself in the original Passover and who had spoken from Mount Sinai.

4. **A corrupted version of Israel's faith will be punished with inescapable exile** (5:27). Amos has warned them that God's judgement will not show favouritism to Israel. Now verse 27 (corresponding to 5:18–19) comes back to his same warning of inescapable judgement if Israel will not change.

'And I will send you into banishment beyond Damascus – says He whose name is Yahweh, the Almighty God' (5:27). The people of Israel loved to think about 'the last things'. Religious people everywhere like to claim that their religion enables them to make predictions concerning the future. Such 'prophecies' are generally flattering to the people that make them. 'God is going to bless us', they say. 'The Day of Yahweh will be wonderful; God will exalt Israel above the nations'. The people loved talk about predictive prophecy, just as they loved the wonderful worship-services at Bethel and Gilgal and Beersheba. Their society was corrupt; their religion was self-pleasing and self-centred.

Amos says 'No! The Day of Yahweh for you will be an exile that will never be reversed and that will lead to the extermination of northern Israel' – unless you change immediately and drastically.

Amos 5:24 is the central focus of this unit of the prophecy. Amos is looking for an abundance of righteousness. It is not a little trickle he wants or a dribble or a splash. He wants their justice to be like the streams that pour down an abundance of water after the coming of the rains. He wants the people of God to be flooded with ever-flowing righteousness like those few rivers in Israel which continue to flow throughout the year even in the times of summer drought. Any other kind of 'religion' will come under his eternal banishment.

Footnotes

[1] The Hebrew has *sikkuth* – the consonants of *Sakkuth* plus the vowels of *shiqquts* ('abomination').
[2] The Hebrew has *kiyyun* – the consonants of *Kaiwan* plus the vowels of *shiqquts* ('abomination').

Chapter 26

Pride and Privilege

(Amos 6:1–6)

Let us try once again to follow the drift of Amos' thought. Amos 1:2–3:8 made the point that God's anger was getting close to the stage where God would not turn back from judgement. *'For three transgressions . . . and especially for four, I will not reverse my decision'*. There were messages for the nations (1:3–2:3) and for Judah (2:4–5), but Amos went on to show that God's judgement was equally hanging over Israel (2:6–16). Amos 3:1–8 belongs with 1:2–2:16, since it presses firmly upon the reader what was said in chapters 1–2.

In a second major section Amos warns that Israel is about to be exterminated. The nation was full of violence (3:9–12); its religion was powerless (3:13–15); its upper-class citizens were arrogant (4:1–3); its pilgrimages were useless (4:4–5).

Yet, says Amos, God had given them many invitation to return to the ways of righteousness. He had sent the disasters that were threatened in the law of God: famine (4:6), drought (4:7–8), damage to the crops (4:9), plague and defeat (4:10), destruction (4:11). After many warnings God is now giving one last invitation (4:12–13).

Then, because God's annihilating judgement is so close, Amos sings a funeral song over Israel. The sections of the poetry have an A-B-C-D-C-B-A structure.

A. The death-song (5:1–3)
  B. Seeking God but not at the sanctuaries (5:4–5)
    C. You . . . turn justice into bitterness (5:6–7)
      D. He . . . The God who makes changes (5:8–9)
    C. You . . . turn righteousness to bribery (5:10–13)
  B. Seeking God (5:14–15)
A. The death-song (5:16–17)

If – and only if – Israel amends its ways and turns to justice and integrity, then God will call a halt to the funeral.

In another A-B-C-B-A structure Amos calls for a flowing river of righteousness.

A Inescapable judgement in the day of Yahweh (5:18–20)
B. Rejection of worship (5:21–23)
C. Let justice roll (5:24)
B. Rejection of idolatry (5:25–26)
A. Inescapable exile (5:27)

Now Amos 6:1–14 brings the middle section to an end by coming back to the cause of everything: Israel's utter complacency and carelessness despite everything that God has done for them in their previous history. There are two small units of analysis in which Amos looks at their complacent pride (6:1–3) and their carelessness amidst many privileges (6:4–6). Then there are two units of final announcement that the end is near. A calamitous punishment (6:7–11) is at hand, based upon the certain principle that God cannot indefinitely ignore the sin of His people (6:12–14).

1. **Complacent pride**. First of all Amos denounces the ease and complacency of Israel's life (6:1).

'Woe to you who live in easy luxury in Zion,
woe to those who feel secure in Samaria,
the distinguished men of the foremost of the
nations,
to whom the house of Israel apply for help.' (6:1)

The two cities, Zion or Jerusalem, and Samaria, were the capitals of Judah and northern Israel. In both countries the upper classes were living a life of laziness and luxury.

Behind the spiritual laziness was pride. They thought the two parts of Israel were *'the foremost of the nations'* and they were *'distinguished men'* within it. 'Ruling classes' are a fact of life in every country, but when such people turn their privileges into a matter of pride rather than responsibility, God's judgement hangs over them But – says Amos – Israel is no better than other cities (6:2). (Despite some expositors, there is nothing in the text that signals verse 2 is a quotation.)

'Go to Calneh and look,
and go from there to Hamath the great.

Then go down to Gath of the Philistines.
Are they better that these kingdoms?
Or is their territory better than yours?' (6:2)

'These kingdoms' seems to refer to Israel and Judah. If religiously and morally Zion and Samaria are decadent, then they will face God's judgement like any other ancient city. Take away Israel's uniqueness as the receiver of a revelation from God – and they are no different from the nations nearby! When the leaders of Israel and Judah reject God's revelation, their lifestyle becomes like that of everyone else. Amos says: if you reject the law of Yahweh then you are identical to the pagan cities of Calneh (a north Syrian city, also spelt as Kullani), Hamath (a powerful city also in the north of Syria) and Gath (the well-known town in Philistia to the south). They too are complacent and lazy! They too are vulnerable to attack. Syria and Philistia have already been condemned by God through Amos's prophecies (1:3–5 condemning Aram or Syria; 1:6–8 condemning Philistia). What is so special about Israel and Judah – once you have taken away obedience to the law of Yahweh? The Israelites think they are 'the foremost of the nations', But Amos asks: are the pagan fortresses to the north and the south any better than Jerusalem and Samaria?

In understanding this verse it is necessary to remember that Amos has already said that Syria and Philistia are doomed to be judged by God. It had not happened yet (although Kullani and Hamath would be devastated a few decades later) but the judgement upon Syria and Philistia had already been announced. Now Amos asks: is there any reason to think Zion and Samaria are any better than these already-condemned countries? Their complacent pride will soon come to an end.

The people of Israel were rejecting Amos's predictions of judgement.

'Do you put off the day of calamity?
But would you bring near a reign of violence?' (6:3)

They put off the evil day that Amos has predicted but bring in a reign of terror for the common people of the land (6:3). Retribution will come sooner or later. Those who have subject others to a reign of terror will face a reign of terror themselves – sent by Yahweh!

2. **Carelessness amidst privilege**. Amos 6:4–6 pictures the self-indulgence of these upper classes.

'Those who recline on beds of ivory
and sprawl on their couches,
and eat lambs from the flock,
and calves from the midst of the stall. (6:4)
They improvise to the sound of the harp,
and like David have composed songs for
themselves. (6:5)
They drink wine from sacrificial bowls,
while they anoint themselves with the finest of oils.
Yet they have not grieved over the ruin of Joseph.' (6:6)

Amos spells out in fuller detail what this indolent life-style involved: lazy luxury (6:4a), delicious dinners (6:4b), marvellous music (6:5), abundant alcohol (6:6a) or one could say 'basins of beer' (6:6a) – but total indifference to the ruin of the nation (6:6b).

Chapter 27

Punishment and Principle

(Amos 6:7–14)

Complacent pride and carelessness amidst privilege is followed by calamitous punishment.

3. **Calamitous punishment**. If the people of Israel and Judah think they are 'the first of the nations', they will be 'the first of the nations' in going into exile (6:7a)! Their feasting will come to a bad end (6:7b).

'Therefore they will now go into exile
as the foremost of the exiles,
and the banqueting of these loungers will pass away.' (6:7)

Amos 6:8 focuses more closely on the underlying pride.

'The sovereign Yahweh has sworn by himself,
– oracle of the Sovereign Yahweh Almighty –
"I loathe the arrogance of Jacob,
and I hate his citadels . . ."' (6:8a)

Pride arouses the anger of God, and the greatest thing He can do in His anger is to take an oath. An oath *'confirms what is said and puts an end to all argument'* (Hebrews 6:16). It is God's final word; no change of plan can take place once it has been given.

What God's punishment will involve is told in fuller detail in 6:8b–10.

'" . . . Therefore I will deliver up the city and everything in it." (6:8b)
And if ten men are left in one house, they will die. (6:9)
Then the nearest relative and the one who burns
the corpse, will lift him up to carry out his body
from the house. The relative will call to anyone
who might be in the innermost parts of the house,

"Is anyone else there with you?" And then he will say, "No one". Then the relative will say, "Keep quiet. For the name of Yahweh is not even to be mentioned."' (6:10)

When relatives come to the scene of disaster after an Assyrian invasion they will find no survivors (6:9–10a). They will call for awed silence at the judgement of God (6:10b) – like Revelation 8:1 when the seventh seal of God's judgement was opened and heaven was stunned for half an hour. The severity and thoroughness of God's punishment is emphasized (6:11).

'For behold, Yahweh will give command
that the great house be smashed to pieces
and the small house to fragments.' (6:11)

Amos says all of this in the name of God, because it is God's last word before it all happens. There is help in the possibility of a last minute change. God is just on the verge of making His very final decision. Yet the very last word has not quite been spoken. God is saying 'I am about to raise up a nation against you' (6:14). Amos is speaking of it because the oath of God (mentioned in 6:8) is just about to be taken. The funeral song is already being sung. Yet if the situation were entirely hopeless God would not be saying anything at all. Once an oath is taken God has nothing more to say! God would not speak to king Saul, after He had made a final decision about him. Jesus would not speak to Herod – his day of opportunity had gone by. While God is speaking to us, there is still hope. 'Today, if you hear His voice, do not harden your heart'. If you no longer hear the voice of God, then that situation has closed down. There is no hope until God speaks again – perhaps about something else or a new plan.

Amos is giving a very last warning. Instant repentance might avert the judgement. Otherwise Israel will come under Assyrian invasion and the nation will cease to exist, only to be taken up again centuries later, in another form.

4. **Certain principle**. As this section comes to a close, and Amos speaks of final and fixed extermination for northern Israel, he puts it in terms of a sure and certain principle. It is settled and incontestable that God will punish sin. Verses

12–13 look at three absurdities: driving horses up a cliff face (6:12a), ploughing the sea with a team of oxen (6:12b), and expecting God to take no notice of poison (6:12c), bitterness (6:12c) and arrogance (6:13). Yahweh will stir up a mighty nation – Assyria – and Israel will go into exile (6:14).

'Do horses run on rocks?
Or does one plough the sea with oxen?[1] (6:12a)

Both ideas are ridiculous suggestions. Yet the point is that it is equally ridiculous to think that God's people can sink so low in sin and injustice and yet nothing be done about it. It is equally ridiculous to think that a country can continue as a 'holy nation' and yet allow such monstrosities as the ill-treatment of the poor, whom God specially loves.

'Yet you have turned justice into poison,
and the fruit of righteousness into wormwood, (6:12b)
you who rejoice in Lo-Debar – A Thing of
Nothing,
you who say "Have we not by our own strength
taken Karmaim – A Pair of Horns – for
ourselves?"' (6:13)

'Wormwood' is the plant, already mentioned in 5:7; it has a bitter taste. 'Lo-Debar' and 'Karnaim' are towns in Transjordania – the area east of the river Jordan. Apparently Israel had recently recaptured them from Syria. But the names of the towns have meanings. 'Lo-Debar' could be translated 'A Thing of Nothing', 'Karmaim' has the meaning 'A Pair of Horns'. So the people of Israel were rejoicing in their military successes.

But their recent successes mean nothing. 'Lo-Debar' is exactly that, 'A Thing of Nothing'. They might think that they are so clever as to have captured a powerful town – 'A Pair of Horns'. But God will have the last word. Will they be able to cope with the might of Assyria coming against them?

'"For behold I am about to raise up a nation
against you"
– oracle of Yahweh God Almighty –
"and they will afflict you from the gateway of
Hamath
to the brook of the Arabah."' (6:14)

The 'gateway of Hamath' was in the extreme north; the 'Arabah' was in the south. The entire country will be afflicted and deported. Pride, social carelessness, arrogant self-confidence, affluent indolence – they are all certain to be punished. It is a mercy to them that Amos is giving them a last warning. The hatred of such sin and the certainty of its arousing God's anger is a fixed and certain principle in God's dealings with the world. His judgement might be slow in coming, but it will surely come. Upon 'Israel', a nation uniquely chosen by God, the judgement is even more certain. For God will not tolerate for long such sin in His people.

Footnote

[1] The Hebrew text could be translated 'Can one plough it with oxen?' but it is likely that the Hebrew *bbqrym* ('with oxen') should be read as two words, *bbqr ym* ('the sea with oxen').

Chapter 28

Amos the Intercessor

(Amos 7:1–9)

The end of Amos chapter 6 leaves us somewhat stunned and awed. The greatness of God's judgement is almost overwhelming. With great houses and small houses smashed to pieces (6:11) and bereaved relatives retreating into stunned silence and fear of even whispering the name of Yahweh. What disaster sin brings! *'Sin, when it is full-grown, brings forth death'* (James 1:15).

Now Amos 7:1–9:15 will tackle the question: is this the last word or is there any hope whatsoever for Israel?

Amos 7:1–9 brings before us three visions. In the first two Israel is faced with the threat of extermination, first by locusts and then by divine fire. In both of the visions the threat of extermination is turned aside by Amos's intercession.

The first vision is a threat of extermination by natural means, that is by a locust invasion.

'This is what the sovereign Yahweh showed me. He was preparing a swarm of locusts at the beginning of the growth of the spring crops. It was the spring crop after the king's share has been harvested' (7:1). The threat of judgement was coming from God. *'And when they had finished consuming the vegetation of the land...'* The judgement was about to be total, a judgement involving complete annihilation. *'And when they had finished consuming the vegetation of the land, I said, "Sovereign Yahweh, please forgive! How can Jacob survive? He is so small"'* (7:2). Amos is a man of intercession; and God heard his praying. *'Yahweh changed His mind concerning this. "It shall not be", said Yahweh'* (7:3).

The second vision is a threat of extermination by supernatural means, that is by divine fire.

'This is what the sovereign Yahweh showed me. The sovereign Yahweh was calling for judgement by fire. It consumed the great deep and it was consuming the land' (7:4). Again the judgement was about to be total. God's holy fire, God fiery holiness, irresistibly devours and eventually annihilates all that is not pleasing to Him. That which does the will of God abides for ever. That which displeased Him is burned up and devoured. This divine fire even devours the ocean; then it was about to proceed to the land. Soon nothing would be left.

But again Amos is a man of intercession. *'And I said, "Sovereign Yahweh, please forgive! How can Jacob survive? He is so small"'* (7:5). And again the Lord heard his prayer, and judgement was averted. *'Yahweh changed His mind concerning this. "It also shall not be", said sovereign Yahweh'* (7:6).

The third vision presents us with a threat of extermination but one that cannot be turned aside by intercession. Twice God had threatened to punish and exterminate Israel. Twice intercession had turned aside the judgement, but now there comes something that apparently cannot be turned aside by judgement. *'This is what He showed me. The sovereign Yahweh was standing beside a wall made with a plumb-line, and He had a plumb-line in His hand'* (7:7). In the vision God was standing by a wall which originally had been made with a plumb-line. In other words when the wall had originally been made, it had been made upright. Now God the Builder is returning to see whether the wall is as upright as it was when He made it. The Builder is returning to check whether the wall is beginning to fall down or whether it is still upright as He made it originally.

God is about to come to Israel and see whether the people of God are still the way He made them in the beginning. *'And Yahweh said to me, "What are you seeing Amos?". And I said "A plumb-line". And the Lord said, "Behold I am about to put a plumb-line among my people Israel; I will spare them no longer"'* (7:8). When God originally redeemed Israel by the blood of the lamb, He then took them to Sinai and gave them His law. On Mount Sinai, the people said *'All that Yahweh has commanded we shall do'* (Exodus 19:8). The originally 'vertical' nation was a nation free from idolatry, worshipping Yahweh only. It was to be a compassionate nation; it had divine laws which protected the poor and led the nation in the direction of compassion and mercy and justice. But now God returns with a plumb-line in His hand. He wants to know whether Israel is still the same as He had made it.

But since the nation is so far removed from the way God had set it up at the beginning, God will destroy it – and this time there can be no intercession.

> *'"The high places of Isaac will be destroyed,*
> *and the sanctuaries of Israel will be ruined;*
> *I will rise against the house of Jeroboam with the sword."'* (7:9)

Why is there no intercession this time? Because Israel's sin has reached the point where even intercession will be useless. Samuel was famous as an intercessor but after Saul's sin of 1 Samuel 15, he made no attempt to see Saul or pray for him. There came a point in the threats against Judah when God said 'Even if Moses and Samuel were to stand before me, my heart would not go out to this people' (Jeremiah 15:1). Jeremiah was told *'Do not pray for this people'* (Jeremiah 11:14). The author of Hebrews knew that there were certain people he could not renew to repentance (Hebrews 6:6); he had nothing to say to them and only spoke to those who had not sunk so low (Hebrews 6:9). John spoke of a *'sin unto death'* and said *'I do not say that anyone should pray for this'* (1 John 5:16). This time Amos cannot report that intercession turned aside God's judgement. There can come sin where intercession will not make any difference, when the prophet cannot renew the people to repentance, where one need not recommend prayer.

What was it that brought the wrath of God upon Israel to this extreme extent where even intercession could not avert the judgement? It was the sin of failing to abide by original specifications. The sin of not 'abiding' in what was given by God at the beginning.

Chapter 29

Amos and Amaziah

(Amos 7:10–17)

Prophetic preaching is likely to get us into trouble. By 'prophetic preaching' I mean preaching which is divinely guided and highly applied. Amos's preaching was applied preaching. He did not state the teaching and leave it at that. He applied what he was teaching to the situation and was not afraid to mention names when necessary. To say 'God will judge sin' would not get him into trouble. People would nod their heads in agreement – and think what Amos was saying applied to other people! But to say *'I will rise against the house of Jeroboam with the sword'* (7:9) was more precise and particular. It is not surprising that it brought a reaction..

> *'Then Amaziah, the priest of Bethel sent a message*
> *to Jeroboam king of Israel. "Amos has planned a*
> *rebellion against you, in the heart of Israel. The*
> *land is unable to endure all his words.* (7:10)
> *For this is what Amos has said, 'Jeroboam shall*
> *die by the sword,*
> *and Israel shall certainly go into exile, taken out of*
> *its land."'* (7:11)

1. **Prophets arouse opposition**. *'They persecuted the prophets who were before you'*, said Jesus (Matthew 5:12). *'As an example ... of suffering ... take the prophets who spoke in the name of the Lord'*, said James (in James 5:10).

(i) Amaziah reported the matter to someone he thought could do Amos harm; Jeroboam was told about what Amos had said.

(ii) Amos was taken as being personally hostile to Jeroboam. *'Amos has planned a rebellion against you ... '*. Of course Amos had done no such thing. He had simply preached God's word in a rather detailed manner. He had nothing personally against Jeroboam.

(iii) The impression is given that many people agree with Amaziah. *'The land is unable to endure all his words'*. It gives the impression that hundreds of people are protesting against Amos. When people criticize preaching, they like to pretend that their opinion is shared by dozens of other people. Generally they are exaggerating.

'And Amaziah said to Amos,
"Go, you seer, run away to the land of Judah. Eat
your bread there; prophesy there. (7:12)
But at Bethel you are not to prophesy any more,
for it is the king's sanctuary, and it is a royal
house."' (7:13)

(iv) Amaziah makes use of Amos's Judean nationality. He said to Amos, *'Go, you seer, run away to the land of Judah'*. It was easy to attack Amos as a foreigner.

(v) Amaziah seems to think that Amos is saying what he has said simply to earn money and because he is a 'professional' prophet. *'Eat your bread in Judah'*, he says. He seems to think that Amos is concerned simply about earning a living, and getting bread to eat.

(vi) Like many people in high office, Amaziah dislikes any hint of preaching that seems to criticize 'the establishment' or the 'official' religion of the country. 'Bethel . . . is the king's sanctuary, and it is a royal house' he says. He obviously thinks it is scandalous to say anything against such 'official' places in the life of Israel. But do not kings and official sanctuaries need the truth rather than flattery simply because they are people and places of such prestige.

2. **The truly prophetic preacher stands by God's word despite opposition**. Amaziah imagined he would easily be able to silence Amos, but it turned out to be not as easy as he thought. Prophets are not always so easy to squash. They are willing to suffer for the word of God. They are willing to stand alone if necessary.

'And Amos answered and said to Amaziah,
"I am not a prophet, and I am not the son of a
prophet;

I was a herdsman and I took care of sycamore trees. (7:14)
But Yahweh took me from following the flock
and Yahweh said to me
"Go prophesy to my people Israel."' (7:15)

(i) Amos did not comply with Amaziah's requests. He was not intimidated by threats. He did not apologize or withdraw his teaching. He knew what he said was a word from God and he had no intention of pretending otherwise.

(ii) Amos appealed to divine call. He had not appointed himself to be a prophet. He was quite content to do what he was doing as a shepherd and tree-farmer. But God had called him; God had given him a message for Israel. He was not 'the son of a prophet', that is, a prophet's disciple in training for prophetic ministry. He had a purely 'secular' job when God had abruptly taken him away from his previous work and sent him to Israel. A prophet is a person who knows his or her calling and knows the message that God has given him.

(iii) Amos repeated his message and made it even more offensive!

'"*And now hear the word of Yahweh,*
You are saying, 'You shall not prophesy against Israel,
nor shall you speak against the house of Isaac.' (7:16)
Therefore this is what Yahweh says:
'Your wife will become a prostitute in the city.
Your land will be divided up by a measuring line.
You yourself will die upon unclean soil.
Moreover, Israel shall indeed go from its land into exile.'"' (7:17)

This has all the characteristic of prophetic preaching. It is assured and certain ('*Now hear the word of Yahweh*'). Amos knows that what he is saying is true. It pin-points Amaziah's sin ('*You are saying, "You shall not prophesy . . ."*'). It is predictive and precise, focusing upon wife, family, land and nation. It is capable of being checked in future days. If Amos's prediction does not come true (assuming there is no repentance) Amos will be revealed as a false prophet.

I do not suppose that Amos enjoyed saying such things. We have seen that he had the heart of an intercessor. Although

Israel and Judah were at enmity at this stage of their history, yet Amos repeatedly (7:1–3, 4–6) interceded for the nation of northern Israel. Yet Amos had no choice. Sovereign Yahweh had spoken. A prophet had no choice but to prophesy. (see 3:8). The true prophet stands by God's word.

Chapter 30

The End Is Come

(Amos 8:1–3)

In Amos 1:2–3:8 we saw God as a roaring lion, about to devour Israel and the surrounding nations. God had not quite finally acted but the lion was roaring and was about to pounce.

In Amos 3:9–6:14 the judgement was so close that Amos was already singing the funeral song. Chastening had proved entirely useless. Israel was receiving one last word from God. The situation was not totally closed since Amos was still telling people to seek God. God was portrayed as the Creator-God who could turn darkness into daylight.

Now in Amos 7:1–9:15, the questions are: will Israel receive God's message? Will 'the end' be finally pronounced. And is there any hope for Israel whatsoever?

In the structure of the Book of Amos, Amos 8:1–3 comes in as a reassertion that the nation of Israel is about to come to an end.

In Amos 7:1–9 God twice threatens to exterminate the nation (7:1–3, 4–6). On both occasions, because of Amos's intercession, the threat is turned aside.

Then a third threat is presented (7:7–9). This time there is no possibility of intercession changing the situation. Israel has got so bad that the nation is beyond the reach of rescue by Amos' intercessory prayer. Yet on the other hand there is nothing in 7:7–9 that is quite so serious as the threat of extermination that was in 7:1–6. The question of whether Israel will survive at all is left open at that point. Certainly judgement will come, but will the nation be annihilated, never to rise again? At the end of 7:9 it seems that the situation is hopeless.

Before the question of survival is finally answered, Amos 7:10–8:3 invites us to consider the question: will Israel take any notice of God's word? The answer appears to be: no! A wicked priest fiercely opposes Amos's preaching and does his best to get rid of the prophet (7:10–13). But God's word and God's prophets cannot be removed so easily. Amos stands firm. He insists on his having been called and sent by God (7:14–15). It will be Amaziah who (because of his rejection of God's word) will be banished from Israel – the very thing Amaziah had wanted for Amos. Amaziah will die outside of his land (7:16–17). Now Amos 8:1–3 insists that if there is no receiving of the word of God, then for the moment all hope for Israel is lost. *'The end is come upon my people Israel'.*

So far the structure of the section is as follows.

God's Sovereign Graciousness (7:1–9:15)

1. Judgement without hope of present renewal (7:1–9)
   - Intercession overcomes earthly judgement (7:1–3)
   - Intercession overcomes eternal judgement (7:4–6)
   - Judgement without benefit of intercession (7:7–9)
2. The word of God rejected (7:10–8:3)
   - Amos opposed (7:10–13)
   - Amos a true prophet (7:14–15)
   - Amaziah is doomed (7:16–17)
   - Israel is doomed (8:1–3)

'This is what the sovereign Yahweh showed me.
Look, a basket of ripe fruit. (8:1)
And He said, "What do you see, Amos?" And I said, "A basket of ripe fruit". Then Yahweh said to me,
"The end is come upon My people Israel;
I will not pardon them any more. (8:2)
And the songs of the palace shall be wailings in that day"
– oracle of sovereign Yahweh.
"The dead bodies shall be many;
in every place they shall throw them aside.
Silence!"' (8:3)

The section involves a play on words. 'Ripe' is Hebrew *qayits*; 'end' is Hebrew *qets*. Amos sees a basket of end-of-the-harvest fruit; God sees an end-of-the-harvest people.

1. **There is a pattern of sowing an reaping in God's treatment of His people**. Whatever a person sows, he or she reaps. Whatever a church or nation plants in the life of the community, it will eventually lead to consequences in their experience of God. God is not mocked. It is not possible to sow bad seed without reaping the appropriate harvest. Israel had been sowing seeds of idolatry and injustice. Now the time has come for reaping. When the fruit is ripe, harvest time has arrived.

2. **God is slow to decide when the end has come, slow to insist that harvest-time has arrived**. At the time of Amos' ministry, northern Israel had been deteriorating for centuries. It was Jeroboam I (931–910 BC), the fourth king in the story of Israel, who introduced an idolatry that ruined the life of Israel. He set up 'high places', open-air places of pagan worship. He made non-Levitical priests, who did not descend from the tribe of Levi as was required by God's law (1 Kings 12:31). Now it is the time of the second Jeroboam! The life of Israel has sunk to crime, immorality and injustice. The poor are suffering. Gods of fertility are worshipped. Sanctuaries are crowded with worshippers but they are places of paganism.

Not far away, growing increasingly powerful, was Assyria. The preaching of Amos and Hosea gave Israel one more opportunity to turn to Yahweh. While they were hearing the call to repentance from Amos and from Hosea, the door for recovery was open, but it would not stay open for ever. The seed has been sown; the crop is growing; soon 'the end' will come and harvest time will arrive. There is only one hope and that is to dig up the old seed of wickedness, and plant some new seed altogether!

3. **Eventually a day of reaping arrives**. There comes a time when God refuses to forgive. Individuals may be forgiven, but the nation as a whole reaps the consequences of its centuries of wickedness. At Jeroboam's death his son lasted only six months (2 Kings 15:8). Northern Israel was conquered by the Assyrian enemy. Sargon II of Assyria (722/1–705/4) initiated a scheme of mass deportation. The nation of northern Israel ceased to exist. Repentance would have brought a turn-about, but to continue in the ways of idolatry was fatal. Throughout the long days of Jeroboam the Lord was giving Israel its last

offer of survival. The nation had one generation left before the volcano would erupt. Soon the songs of the palace would become shrieks of distress.

'Silence!' is the last word of Amos 8:3. As in Amos 6:9–10, when relatives who came to the scene of disaster after an Assyrian invasion would call for awed silence, so in the days when Israel reaps after two centuries of sowing, anyone who witnesses 'the end' will stand still in awed silence at the severity and thoroughness of God's closing judgement.

Is there any escape from this? Only for individuals. If any one person will hear Amos's voice and open the doorway of faith in Yahweh and His promises, there will be salvation for that one individual – but the nation as a whole is about to come to its end. Amidst the darkest judgement God can protect individuals but – says Amos – northern Israel will soon cease to exist in the form that it had been known.

The good news for us is that the sowing and reaping can be the other way around. If bad seed reaps its harvest, so does good seed. If those who sow to the flesh reap disaster, equally those who sow to the Spirit reap the blessings of eternal life. The question is: what are we sowing. Everyone 'ripens' as time goes by. Sooner or later, everyone gets to be ripe for judgement or ripe for God's blessing. The question is: which one will it be?

Chapter 31

Judgement Without Recovery

(Amos 8:4–10)

We have been looking at the structure of Amos 7:1–9:15. The entire section may be entitled: God's Sovereign Graciousness (7:1–9:15). The questions that are being put to us are: will Israel survive at all? Is there any hope of Israel's receiving God's Word? We have had sections which might be entitled:

1. Judgement without hope of present renewal (7:1–9)
2. The word of God rejected (7:10–8:3)

Now in a small central unit (8:4–10), Amos again gives the reason for Israel's imminent end. It is a matter of just retribution. Crime is being followed by punishment. The next section may again be entitled:

3. Crime and punishment (8:4–10).

Amos 8:4–6 lists the crimes. Amos 8:7–10 speaks of the oath of God in which He determines to bring the situation to an end.

We may now take a look ahead at Amos 8:11–9:15. The hope for Israel is in the fact that Amos is preaching to the nation. While God is speaking to us there is hope of recovery. But Amaziah, and the nation generally, have rejected Amos's word. So the word that has been opposed will for the moment be lost in Israel. Amos 8:11–9:6 describes a situation in which a famine of hearing the word of God settles upon the nation. The section may be entitled: the word of God lost (8:11–9:6). This brings us more acutely than ever to the question: is there any hope for Israel at all?

Amos 9:7–15 answers the question. God will *'destroy it from the face of the earth'* but *'nevertheless* [He] *will not totally destroy the house of Jacob'*. With all other nations, Israel will be thoroughly shaken and many sinners will be removed altogether (9:7–10). But there is one note of hope: the house of David! The only hope for northern Israel is not in northern Israel at all but in Amos's own Judah! Israel may at some undated future time recover – but only through the house of David (9:11–15).

So it now appears that the structure of Amos 7:1–9:15 once again follows the A-B-C-B-A pattern much loved by Amos.

A. Judgement – without hope of present renewal (7:1–9)
B. The word of God rejected (7:10–8:3)
C. Crime and punishment (8:4–10)
B. The word of God lost (8:11–9:6)
A. Judgement – with hope of future renewal (9:7–15).

Amos 7:1–9 balances 9:7–15 and deals with a similar topic. Amos 7:10–8:3 balances 8:11–9:6 and deals with a similar topic. Amos 8:4–10 is a centre-piece of the section. Let us consider it in fuller detail.

1. **Amos again lists the crimes of Israel**. The upper classes of Israel put their own greed above every claim of mercy towards people, every claim of reverence towards God.

'Hear this, you who trample upon the needy,
and bring the poor of the land to an end, (8:4)
you who say, "When will the new moon be finished,
so that we may sell grain,
and when will the Sabbath come to an end,
so that we may offer wheat for sale?"
You who reduce the quantity, the ephah,
but raise the price, the shekel,
who cheat with false scales, (8:5)
who buy the needy for silver,
and the poor for a pair of sandals.
You want to sell even the husks of grain.' (8:6)

The crimes that aroused God to anger were (i) domineering over the poor (*'you who trample upon the needy'*), (ii) eliminating them from any position in society (*'you who ... bring the poor ... to an end'*), (iii) showing such greed for money-making that they could hardly wait for their idolatrous religion to be finished so that they could get on with more money-making (8:4a), (iv) showing dishonesty in their business-methods (8:4b), (v) unrelentingly oppressing the poor (8:5).

2. **Pride brings down God's judgement**. A time of irreversible judgement is at hand, says Amos.

> *'Yahweh has sworn by the "Pride" of Jacob, "I will never forget any of their misdeeds."'* (8:7)

The 'pride of Jacob' could be taken in four ways. (i) One scholar thinks it refers to the land of Israel; I personally doubt it. (ii) Some think the Hebrew means *'against the pride of Jacob'*; this would be an unprecedented meaning for a common Hebrew phrase meaning 'swear by'. (iii) It could be sarcasm. The 'pride' of Jacob is so steadfast you can take an oath by it! (iv) 'Pride of Jacob' could be taken as a title for God (like 'Mighty One of Jacob' in Genesis 49:24). If the fourth option is right (as I believe) it deliberately picks up from what was said in 6:8. God swear's against Israel's pride; He swears by His own pride! Once God has taken an oath, the judgement is unalterably certain. God now swears not to forget their sin but to punish it in a way that will never be reversed. When northern Israel was devastated by the Assyrians it would be a judgement that would never be precisely undone. Northern Israel never recovered. What brought down the extermination of the nation was pride. Some sins are more fatal than others; pride is one of them.

> *'"For this reason should not the land tremble,*
> *and should not everyone who lives in it mourn?*
> *The whole land will rise like the Nile;*
> *it will be tossed about and sink again,*
> *like the river of Egypt.* (8:8)
> *And it shall happen on that day"*
> *– oracle of the sovereign Yahweh -*
> *"I will make the sun go down at noon;*
> *I will darken the earth in the clear daylight."'* (8:9)

The judgement will be like an earthquake, a flood and an eclipse combined! The land will shake. God's judgement will come in like a flood, like the overflowing Nile. The land will be shaken up and down. The sun will disappear. It is no doubt picture-language, but it pictures destructive, overwhelming, frightening judgement. The literal earthquake two years after

Amos's preaching (see 1:1) must have given the people a reminder of what Amos said!

> '"*I will turn your festivals into mourning,*
> *and all your songs in a lamentation.*
> *I will bring sackcloth upon every pair of thighs;*
> *I will shave your heads.*
> *I will make it to be like a time of mourning for an*
> *only son,*
> *and its outcome like a bitter day.*"' (8:10)

Festivities will be turned to mourning. People will put on sackcloth, and go around with shaved heads – both signs of grief. It will be like a bitter bereavement.

Amos's words are almost without hope. If God has – or is about to – swear an oath, what hope can there be? It is a measure of the powerful devastation and destruction that pride brings. There is almost no hope for Israel if the nation will not repent of its pride. If there is ever to be any hope for Israel, it will have to be like a resurrection from death. Pride is so destructive, its end is ruin with almost no hope of recovery.

Chapter 32

The Lost Word

(Amos 8:11–9:6)

If in Israel the word of God is not heeded, then one aspect of God's punishment is that the ability to hear God's word will be lost.

1. **The loss of the genuine** (8:11–12). When the word is rejected there comes an inability to hear it.

'"Behold the days are coming" – oracle of
sovereign Yahweh –
"when I will send a famine on the land,
not a famine for bread or a thirst for water,
but a famine of hearing of Yahweh's words. (8:11)
They shall wander from sea to sea,
from north to east.
They will run here and there to seek the word of
Yahweh –
but they shall not find it."' (8:12)

Amos does not precisely say there would be a famine of the word. That might be true as well but what Amos says is that there would be a famine of the hearing of the Word. Refusal to hear the word results in inability to hear the word. And that leads to instability and confusion. The people will go *'from sea to sea'*. The Dead Sea was in the south; the Mediterranean was in the west. They go eastward and northward as well. They look everywhere for a source of guidance but they do not hear any word from God, because they are unable to do so.

2. **The uselessness of the false** (8:13–15). In the day when the hearing of God's word has been lost, a generation will arise which is unaware that it has lost anything. Yet the consequences of the lost word will appear.

'"In that day beautiful girls will faint,
and the finest young men will faint from thirst."' (8:13)

The terms speak of young people. When the word is lost the upcoming generation know no better than to turn to the popular gods of the day. It was fashionable to swear by a god whose name was Ashimah; the name was similar to the Hebrew word for 'guilt' and Amos makes use of the fact. Also it seems that it was popular to swear by the blessings that were thought to come from a pilgrimage to Beersheba.

'"Those who swear by the Guilt of Samaria,
whose who say 'As your god lives, O Dan'
or 'As the way of Beersheba lives' –
they shall fall and never rise again."' (8:14)

But the cults from Assyria which were attracting young people were drawing them into superstition, not into the life of godliness. As a result the entire community would be doomed. Soon the Assyrian armies would arrive and the entire northern nation would be swept away. These young people like everyone else would *'fall and never rise again'*. The inability to hear God's word was fatal. Without God's word there can be no saving experience of God. Religious superstition is a useless replacement for the life of faith. True faith cleanses from sin; religious superstition is designed to get some advantage or happiness from some god. The word of God received brings a knowledge of God. The word of God rejected brings spiritual starvation.

3. **The destruction of the fake** (9:1–6). The useless religion of northern Israel had all begun when Jeroboam the first had set up a self-invented religion in Bethel. He had offered sacrifice himself at the altar (see 1 Kings 12:32). Now two hundred years later, the entire fake religion started by Jeroboam is about to be destroyed. Amos sees a vision. The destruction of Jeroboam's cult has been much delayed, but now its day of judgement has come.

'I saw the sovereign One, standing beside the altar;
and He said,
"Strike the heads of the columns so that the
thresholds may shake!
Smash them on the head, all of them!

Then I will kill the rest of them with the sword.
No fugitive among them will make good his escape;
no refugee among them will survive."' (9:1)

God stands by the altar, just as Jeroboam had once done. But He stands by the altar to destroy it. The entire superstitious temple at Bethel will be destroyed (see 1 Kings 12:31–33). The nation will cease; the people will be killed. The judgement is inescapable if they will not repent – and now is so far gone that it is inescapable even if they do repent, as perhaps some did. Calamitous consequences might follow sin even when it is forgiven.

The catastrophe about to come will be irresistible.

'"Though they dig down into Sheol,
from there my hand shall take them.
Though they climb into heaven,
from there I will bring them down; (9:2)
though they hide themselves on top of Carmel,
from there I will search and take them away.
Though they hide themselves from my sight
in the bottom of the sea,
from there I will command a sea-monster,
and it will consume them."' (9:3)

Nothing can separate them from the wrath of God. Even after they have been exiles to Assyria, God's anger will follow them and there will be further calamities.

'"Even if they go into exile before their enemies,
even there I shall command the sword and it will
kill them.
I shall set my eyes on them, for calamity and not
for good." (9:4)
And sovereign Yahweh, the Almighty,
who touches the land and it melts
and all who dwell in it mourn.
It all rises like the Nile,
and subsides like the river of Egypt.' (9:5)

The God who judges them is the Creator.

'He who built its upper regions in the heavens,
and establishes its lower structures on the earth,
who calls for the waters of the sea,
and pours them on the face of the earth –'

But He is also the Redeemer.

'Yahweh is His name.' (9:6)

The Creator-Redeemer of Israel will become the nation's Judge and Executioner. What was the sin that brought such disaster? Religion without the word of God. Self-appointed religion. Man-made religion. Religion designed to benefit the worshippers with soft living, idle ways, and no great demands. Such a religion is doomed, and its worshippers will perish along with the fake religion.

Chapter 33

Can God's People Cease to Exist?

(Amos 9:7–10)

The question that is now in our minds as we approach the end of Amos's book is: was there any hope for northern Israel whatsoever? As the prophecy has proceeded, the message seems to have become intensely severe. God has taken – or is on the very edge of taking – an oath against Israel (4:12; 6:8; 8:7). Once an oath of anger is taken by God, it cannot be changed or avoided.

Is Israel to be exterminated altogether? Might not God have mercy on a 'remnant' of Israel? This was suggested by Amos 5:15 (*'Perhaps Yahweh, God Almighty, will be gracious to a remnant of Joseph'*). While Philistines will *'perish even to the remnant'* (1:8) and not the slightest remainder of their community will be allowed to survive, perhaps God will preserve a residue of Israelites, a small number that will continue. Maybe a small section of the nation will be allowed to outlast the disaster if they seek Yahweh now before it is too late. Otherwise Amos has sung a funeral song over them.

In this section Amos raises a question: will God allow His people to continue if they lose their distinctiveness?

> *' "Are not you and the Cushites both the same to me –*
> *you people of Israel? Oracle of Yahweh!*
> *Did I not bring Israel up from Egypt*
> *and the Philistines from Caphtor, and the Arameans from Kir?" '* (9:7)

The purpose of God's rescuing Israel from Egypt was to take them to Himself and purify them so that they would become utterly different from the nations of the world. If Israel resembles the other nations in their wicked ways, then there ceases to be anything special about the exodus. God brought Israel out of Egypt. So what? God is moving nations around all the time. He moved the Philistines from Caphtor on the island of Crete. He moved the Arameans from Kir. What is special about the exodus? Nothing at all unless you appreciate the meaning of it; and its meaning is that it was the time when He was taking Israel to Himself to make them different from the other nations. If that 'differentness' is neglected or repudiated, then the exodus loses its significance. It remains a historical fact, like other migrations in the history of the world – but it has no special meaning to us. Take way God's purpose to make Israel unique, and there is no other purpose that can be seen in Israel's departure from Egypt. It becomes just like the Philistine immigration from Caphtor, or the Aramean immigration from Kir.

So if Israel is just like any other nation, and the exodus is just like other migrations among the nations, will God allow His people to continue? Amos answers the question. There are two parts to the answer. (i) **God will destroy Israel** and the nation will not be allowed to continue as it has been for centuries. If northern Israel has totally lost its distinctiveness, then just as 'the Philistines will perish even to the remnant' (1:8), just as *'the Aramean people will go into exile'* (1:5) – might He not say something similar to Israel? He almost says it:

' "Look, the eyes of the sovereign Yahweh
are on the sinful kingdom,
and I will destroy it from the face of the
earth, . . ." '

But actually God has something to add to His prediction.

' ". . . yet I will not totally destroy the house of
Jacob" – oracle of Yahweh.' (9:8)

The destroying, annihilating, exterminating anger of God will almost wipe northern Israel out of existence, but He cannot quite do that. Israel itself had almost destroyed what God had done in making the nation unique, because the nation had ceased to hold to its faith in Yahweh. Israel was ripe for exterminating punishment, like the other nations surrounding Israel. Yet whatever Israel might have done, it was still true to say, 'You only have I known of all the families of the earth'. God could not completely and utterly go back on His choice of Israel. He was swearing – taking an oath – that He would punish Israel; but He had also sworn to Abraham that his seed would last for ever! He could wipe other nations out of existence, but He could not totally and utterly do that with Israel.

(ii) **God judges his people with a discriminating, purifying judgement**.

> *'"For look, I will give the command*
> *and shall shake the house of Israel among all the nations,*
> *as one shakes something in a sieve and not a pebble reaches the ground."'* (9:9)

Amos uses an illustration. He imagines someone sieving out stones or pebbles from sand or soil. (There is no reference to grain; grain was winnowed not sieved.) In Amos's illustration, it is not what falls through the sieve that is destroyed. Rather what gets through the sieve is purified, and what is retained is subsequently thrown away. The large 'pebbles' of the nation will be thrown away. Even those who go into exile will suffer further agonies and will be extinguished from the story of human history. There will no return from the exile of northern Israel. The northern part of the nation will cease to exist. Only a tiny remnant will be purified and will survive. How will they survive? Amos goes on to deal with that in the next few verses. But the bulk of the nation will be wiped out.

> *'"All the sinners among my people will die by the sword,*
> *all who say 'Disaster will not overtake us or meet us.'"'* (9:10)

After the death of Jeroboam II the nation survived for a few decades and then northern Israel was destroyed. It ceased to exist. Amos's predictions were fulfilled. 2 Kings 17:1–18 records the end of northern Israel. The capital city of Samaria was besieged (2 Kings 17:5) and eventually was defeated. The people were deported to far away places in Assyria (17:6). 1 Kings 17:21–23 points out that the removal of the northern kingdom was a fulfilment of prophecy. Were there any survivors? Only a tiny remnant was preserved. They presumably made their way to the southern kingdom of

Judah. There was no hope for Samaria in the immediate future.

God wants His church to be distinctive and sharply different from the world. If at any point His people cease to be a distinctive people, and an unbelieving 'church' arises, that part of His church is abandoned perhaps for centuries. A remnant survive; a new movement of the Spirit takes place elsewhere and the remnant are blessed in the new thing that God does – elsewhere. Whether the old 'shell' that was abandoned will ever be restored is doubtful, but one notes in Scripture that northern Israel became the corrupt, half-Assyrian, half-Israelite 'Samaritans'. They never got any special blessing from God until Jesus came – but then they were the first pagans outside of Israel to be given the gospel. *'You shall be my witnesses in Jerusalem, and in all Judea, and in Samaria!'* (Acts 1:8). Eventually even northern Israel was restored but only in the gospel of Jesus Christ.

Chapter 34

The Hope of the Future

(Amos 9:11–15)

The note of hope in the message of Amos is so surprising to some people that they think Amos could not have written it. Yet if this message of hope contradicted Amos, why was anyone so crazy as to make a book contradict itself without smoothing out the contradiction? If it does not contradict Amos, then why could Amos himself not have written it? The words of Amos 9:11–15 are Amos's words.

1. **The hope for northern Israel was to be found in the south**. The only hope for 'the remnant' that might not come under God's judgement would be for them to join Judah in the south.

> '"*In that day I will raise up the collapsed hut, the house of David;*
> *I will repair the cracks in it, and restore it from its ruins;*
> *I will rebuild it as in the days of old.*"' (9:11)

God gave promises to David. A Saviour for Israel would come in the line of David. But in the days of Jeroboam I, northern Israel broke away and turned to idolatry. The northern nation continued for two centuries more. It fell into greater sin than ever in the days of Jeroboam II (in Amos's time), and then in 721 BC ceased to exist. Jeroboam's experiment with idolatry totally failed.

The only hope for any survivors was to turn to David's kingdom again! The 'house of David' was still on the throne in the south. The line of King David would continue until the Saviour came. Salvation would come from the Judeans!

Amos gives predictions about the only hope for Israel – in the southern house of David. 'That day' is the unexplained, undated future. Amos's prophetic viewpoint looks forward to everything God would do in His saving plans. He looks into the undated future and sees, in one sweeping picture, the salvation that God will bring to the entire world.

Much sin was to be found in Judah as well as in Israel (as Amos said back in 2:4–5). We – from a later vantage point – know that Judah also will be exiled to Babylon, yet the Judeans will survive in a way that will not be the case with northern Israel. The line of David will continue even when the Davidic kings are no longer sitting on the throne. The house of David was in Amos's time like a ruined and broken down house. But one day God will restore it! A Saviour will come. A 'house' for God to dwell in will be raised up. Amos does not say quite how this will happen, but the fulfilment made it clear. Jesus came in the line of David. The Holy Spirit was poured out on three thousand Judeans, and the kingdom of God was magnificently restored in the church of Jesus Christ. Even that is not the end of the story for we have reason to believe that modern 'Israel' will eventually join the church of Jesus Christ (Romans 11:26 should, I believe, be taken this way).

2. **Amos expects a day of restoration and magnificent expansion**. In the 8th century BC he looks to a coming blessing in the house of David. Its beginnings are over seven hundred years ahead.

> *'"The result will be that they will possess what is*
> *left of Edom,*
> *and will possess all the nations over whom My*
> *name has been pronounced."*
> *Oracle of Yahweh! He will do it!'* (9:12)

When the day comes for Israel's restoration, even the traditional enemies of Israel will be added to the newly restored people of God. Israel will even take over Edom – their traditional enemies who had hated them for centuries! And all other nations will be added to God's Israel as well.

The modern Christian can see how it has happened. Israel was 'restored' on the day of Pentecost, and soon thousands of Gentiles were joining God's restored 'Israel', the church. 'Israel' began with a remnant of Jews but thousands and now millions of Gentiles were engrafted into God's 'Israel'.

The word 'Israel' has more than one meaning, but its main meaning is that it is the people of God, originally to be found within one nation but now a multinational body of people, the church of Jesus Christ.

Amos 9:11–12 was quoted by James at the Council of Jerusalem (see Acts 15:16–17). Detailed comment on this belongs more to an exposition of Acts than of Amos, since James' words echo words from Hosea, Jeremiah and Isaiah, as well as Amos. James was referring to more than Amos alone. However James' main points are in the Hebrew text of Amos, as well as in the 'expository' translation to be found in the Greek Old Testament.

The Greek version of this text may be translated as follows:

'"In that day I will raise up the fallen tabernacle
of David,
and I will rebuild its ruins and raise up its parts,
and I will rebuild it as in the days of previous ages,
so that what remains of men and all the nations
over whom My name is called may seek Me,"
says the Lord who does all these things.'

James (in Acts 15:16–17) quotes it in his own way:

'"After this I will return and I will rebuild the fallen tabernacle of David, and its ruins I shall rebuild and I shall set it up, so that what remains of men may seek the Lord, and all the Gentiles over whom My name is called, says the Lord who does these things known from of old."'

It can be seen that James is roughly (but not exactly) quoting the Greek translation of Amos 9:11–12. The opening words (*'After this'*) and the closing words (*'known from of old'*) do not exactly come from Amos. The quotation echoes Hosea 3:5, Jeremiah 12:15 and Isaiah 45:21, as well.

The Greek translation reads 'adam' (men) instead of 'Edom'. This does not greatly change the meaning, so James does not bother to correct the translation he is using, the Greek one. The idea that the argument depends on the reading of the Greek text is not right. The Hebrew makes the same point, and (although saying 'Edom' rather that 'men') equally predicts the entry of Gentiles into the church.

One must keep in mind the biblical idea of 'Israel'. God's

people are at first a family (Abraham's clan), then a nation of believers. All Israelites as a whole had faith in the blood of the lamb and crossed the 'Sea of Reeds' by faith (Hebrews 11:29). But in the later generations, *'Not all are Israel who have descended from Israel'*. God's people become a 'remnant' within the nation of Israel. Then after the outpouring of the Spirit, Gentiles are added to God's 'remnant' Israel. Non-Jews become part of 'Israel'. God's 'Israel' equals remnant-Israel plus saved Gentiles. Even people who have hated God's people – spiritual 'Edomites' – are turned around and added to God's 'Israel'. And the story has not ended, for one day (Romans 11:26) 'national' Israel' will turn in faith to Jesus and join God's 'spiritual' Israel. What great days are ahead for the church of Jesus Christ!

Chapter 35

The New World

(Amos 9:13–15)

Old Testament prophecy is often 'panoramic'. What I mean by that is that it sees a full outline of God's future plans in one sweep, without making differentiation into distinct epochs of time. Or a Christian might say 'Old Testament prophecy often deals with the first coming and the second coming of Jesus, all in one breath'. So it is in Amos 9:11–15. It takes in what we now know to be the coming of Jesus to Israel, the outpouring of the Spirit upon the Gentiles and – as we now see – the new heavens and new earth in which righteousness makes its home. The vision takes in everything in one sweep; the fulfilment unfolds in stages.

' "The days are coming" – oracle of Yahweh –
"when the ploughman will overtake the reaper,
and the one who treads on the grapes
will overtake the one who sows the seed.
The mountains shall drip with sweet wine,
all the hills shall flow with it." ' (9:13)

It is a picture of material paradise. The ultimate blessing that God will bring upon His 'Israel' – the entire people of God – is one of earthly glory, paradise restored, new heavens and a new earth in which righteousness dwells. Amos pictures that new world as one in which there is so much agricultural prosperity that the people reaping the crops are gathering vast quantities of produce, and when the next season starts, they have not finished gathering in the vast quantities from the previous harvest. The people crushing the grapes to make wine are still at work when the time for sowing the seed comes round again. The mountains and hills are 'dripping' with prosperity and abundance.

It is a beautiful picture. How literal it is we do not know. We shall find out when we get to the new heavens and new earth. When will it happen? It is not given to us to know the 'times and the seasons'. It is certain that our final reward will be an earthly one. The Christian's final 'heaven' will not be a matter of floating around in space like a ghost or a bodiless angel. The new Jerusalem comes down upon the earth. We shall have glorified bodies and live in a glorified physical world. Is this picture fulfilled then, or might some of this picture be fulfilled even before Jesus comes? One thing is sure: if it comes within the gospel age it will be the result of preaching the gospel. God's 'restorations' do not come in any other way than by the gospel of our Lord Jesus Christ.

'"I shall restore the fortunes of my people Israel,
and they shall rebuild the ruined cities and live in them.
They shall plant vineyards and drink their wine,
they will lay out gardens and eat their fruit. (9:14)
I shall plant them in their own land,
and they shall never again be uprooted
out of the land that I have given them."
Oracle of Yahweh, your God.' (9:15)

We have seen the biblical idea of 'Israel'. The church today, God's 'Israel', consists of remnant-Israel plus saved Gentiles. One day 'national' Israel' will join God's 'spiritual' Israel.

God will restore the fortunes of His people 'Israel'. At the time Amos wrote, 'Israel' was about to be almost annihilated. It would never be the same again. The northern territory would be full of pagans and Samaritans. But that did not mean God had given up on His 'Israel'. No; some northerners would join Judah. One day the Son of David would be sent to die on a cross. The Holy Spirit would be poured out. God would restore the fortunes of His people 'Israel'.

What sort of 'Israel' is in mind here? *'I shall plant them in their own land, and they shall never again be uprooted out of the land that I have given them'*. This will certainly happen in the world to come, the new heavens and new earth which comes down out of heaven.

Today, as I write, the earthly nation of Israel is back in some of its ancient territory. Is this the fulfilment of Amos's prophecy? Well, the return of the nation of Israel to its ancient territory – an event that came about through various political episodes beginning in 1917 – is certainly interesting. But it needs to be said that those events are only a vague foreshadowing of something much bigger that God is planning. The people of Israel are not saved yet, in any vast numbers. They are as paganised as they were in the days of Amos. A much greater blessing is in store for the whole world, much greater than any political scheme that arose in 1917. Amos's prediction has to do with the gospel of the Lord Jesus Christ, rather than the schemes of secularised politicians.

The day when God's total Israel are settled in 'their own land' 'never again ... uprooted' will come in a much richer and fuller way. God has promised us 'new heavens and a new earth in which righteousness has its dwelling-place'. Those who live for God will enjoy a new home altogether. It will quite literally be 'heaven on earth'. Heaven will become earthly; the new Jerusalem will come down on to the earth. In the Bible, sometimes our future home is pictured as a garden, sometimes it is pictured as a city, sometimes it is pictured as a marriage-festival, sometimes it is pictured as home. We shall dwell with God. The new world will be the home of righteousness, a place of peace, joy, worship, fellowship, and of restful activity. It will be a place of love, a reconstructed world. Noisily and dramatically the world in its present form will cease to be. It does not mean that all material existence is brought to an end. The saved will live in a renovated planet. But the world in its old sin-dominated form is brought to an end. The new heavens and new earth of 2 Peter 3:13 is a world newly created from the ashes of the old world.

The 'Israel' north of Judah would soon after Amos's time be utterly destroyed, but there is a day coming when God's enlarged Israel will be settled in their own land, never to be uprooted. Heaven on earth will soon come to the whole of God's people. It is an *'oracle of Yahweh, your God'*; it will certainly happen, maybe sooner than we think.

If you have enjoyed this book and would like to help us to send a copy of it and many other titles to needy pastors in the **Third World**, please write for further information or send your gift to:

Sovereign World Trust
PO Box 777, Tonbridge
Kent TN11 0ZS
United Kingdom

or to the **'Sovereign World'** distributor in your country.